W. Davenport (William Davenport) Goforth, William J. (William John) McAuley

Old colonial architectural details in and around Philadelphia

50 plates of scaled and measured drawings

W. Davenport (William Davenport) Goforth, William J. (William John) McAuley

Old colonial architectural details in and around Philadelphia
50 plates of scaled and measured drawings

ISBN/EAN: 9783742891624

Manufactured in Europe, USA, Canada, Australia, Japa

Cover: Foto ©ninafisch / pixelio.de

Manufactured and distributed by brebook publishing software (www.brebook.com)

W. Davenport (William Davenport) Goforth, William J. (William John) McAuley

Old colonial architectural details in and around Philadelphia

Details

IN AND AROUND

Philadelphia.

80 PLATES OF SCALED AND MEASURED DRAWINGS

BY

W. Davenport Goforth

AND

William J. McAuley,

Architects.

COPYRIGHTED 1890.

NEW YORK:

WM. HELBURN,

65 E. 9th STREET.

PREFACE.

WE desire here to state, that our endeavors have been to collect as good specimens of "OLD COLONIAL ARCHITECTURAL DETAILS" of their respective classes, as could be found in and around PHILADELPHIA.

The plates are arranged as nearly as possible in Historical order.

In the early part of the work we were assisted by Mr. HOWARD S. RICHARD, Archit, who was compelled to retire on account of the pressure of other business.

WM. DAVENPORT GOFORTH.
WILLIAM J. McAULEY.

PHILADELPHIA, Oct. 31st, 1890.

LIST OF CONTENTS.

PLATE 1.
Independence Hall. Built 1729. One-half Elevation of Main Corridor.

PLATE 2.
Detail of Main Corridor, showing Entablature.

PLATE 3.
Detail of Corridor, showing Finish over Doors.

PLATE 4.
Detail of Tablet in Corridor.

PLATE 5.
Elevation and Detail of Tablet containing Declaration of Independence.

PLATE 6.
Urn on Independence Hall. Cornices on Mayor's Office and House, Leonhard Street, below Fourth, Philadelphia.

PLATE 7.
Thomas Mansion. 1754. One-half Elevation and Detail of Drawing-Room.

PLATE 8.
Elevation and Plan of Stair-Hall, showing Window-Seat.

PLATE 9.
Side Elevation and Detail of Stairs.

PLATE 10.
Elevation of Lintel, First Floor Hall, and Details of Window and Cornice in Halls, Second and Third Floor.

PLATE 11.
Elevation and Detail of Window, First Landing of Stairs. Detail of Window Trim and Wainscot Caps, Second Floor.

PLATE 12.
Elevation and Detail of Door and Window, First Floor.

PLATE 13.
Outside Cornice of Thomas Mansion and Door, Window Trim and Sill, and Coping of Wall, Stenton.

PLATE 14.
Arnold Mansion. Built 1763. One-half Elevation of Drawing-Room. Entire Side of Room Oak.

PLATE 15.
Elevation of Door, and Detail of Door, Wainscot Caps and Window Trims.

PLATE 16.
Elevation of Lintel. Detail of Lintel, Cornice and Wainscoting.

PLATE 17.
Elevation and Detail of Half-Window, Second Floor.

PLATE 18.
One-half Elevation of Lintel. Detail of Lintel, Cornice and Wainscoting, First Floor.

PLATE 19.
Fisher Mansion. Built about 1770. Elevation and Detail of Porch.

PLATE 20.
Detail of Stairs and Wainscot, First and Second Floor. Detail of Wainscoard and Window Trims.

PLATE 21.
Elevation and Detail of Fire-Place in Drawing-Room. Hazard Mansion.

PLATE 22.
Elevation and Detail of Door and Window in Drawing-Room.

PLATE 23.
One-half Elevation and Detail of Back Drawing-Room.

PLATE 24.
Elevation and Detail of Lintel of First Floor Hall, and Detail of Drawing-Room Cornice.

PLATE 25.
Elevation and Detail of Fire-Place in Drawing-Room.

PLATE 26.
Hamilton Mansion. Woodlands. Elevation and Detail of Rear Facade.

PLATE 27.
Elevation and Detail of Door in Rear Facade.

PLATE 28.
Elevation and Detail of Fire-Place.

PLATE 29.
Elevation and Detail of Window.

PLATE 30.
Wister House, Fourth, below Spruce Street. Elevation and Detail of Doorway.

PLATE 31.
Wister House, Germantown. Elevation and Detail of Fire-Place.

PLATE 32.

Fyes Mansion, Belmont, Elevation and Detail of Fire Place.

PLATE 33.

Pennsylvania Society Building, Elevation and Detail of Main Entrance.

PLATE 34.

Elevation and Detail of Doorway of Dr. Denton's House, Germantown.

PLATE 35.

Elevation and Sections of Two Outside Cornices.

PLATE 36.

Elevation and Plan of Old Doorway, Fifth and Powell Streets, Philadelphia.

PLATE 37.

Detail of Entablature of Doorway, Fifth and Powell Streets.

PLATE 38.

Detail of Spandrel, Panel Molding and Horizontal Section Through Side Light, Fifth and Powell Streets.

PLATE 39.

Elevation and Detail of Fire Place, Germantown.

PLATE 40.

Elevation and Detail of Doorway, Union Street, above Third, Philadelphia.

PLATE 41.

Elevation and Detail of Doorway, Locust Street, below Fifth, Philadelphia.

PLATE 42.

Elevation and Detail of Doorway, Germantown.

PLATE 43.

Elevation and Detail of Fire-Place, Woodford Mansion.

PLATE 44.

Elevation and Detail of Fire-Place in Dr. Garrett's Residence, Germantown.

PLATE 45.

Two Inside Cornices.

PLATE 46.

Detail of Door and Window Trims, Cornice, Wainscot and Wash-Board.

PLATE 47.

Balusters and Hand-Rails.

PLATE 48.

Gate, Balcony and Newel Posts.

PLATE 49.

Fan and Side Lights.

PLATE 50.

Fan Lights.

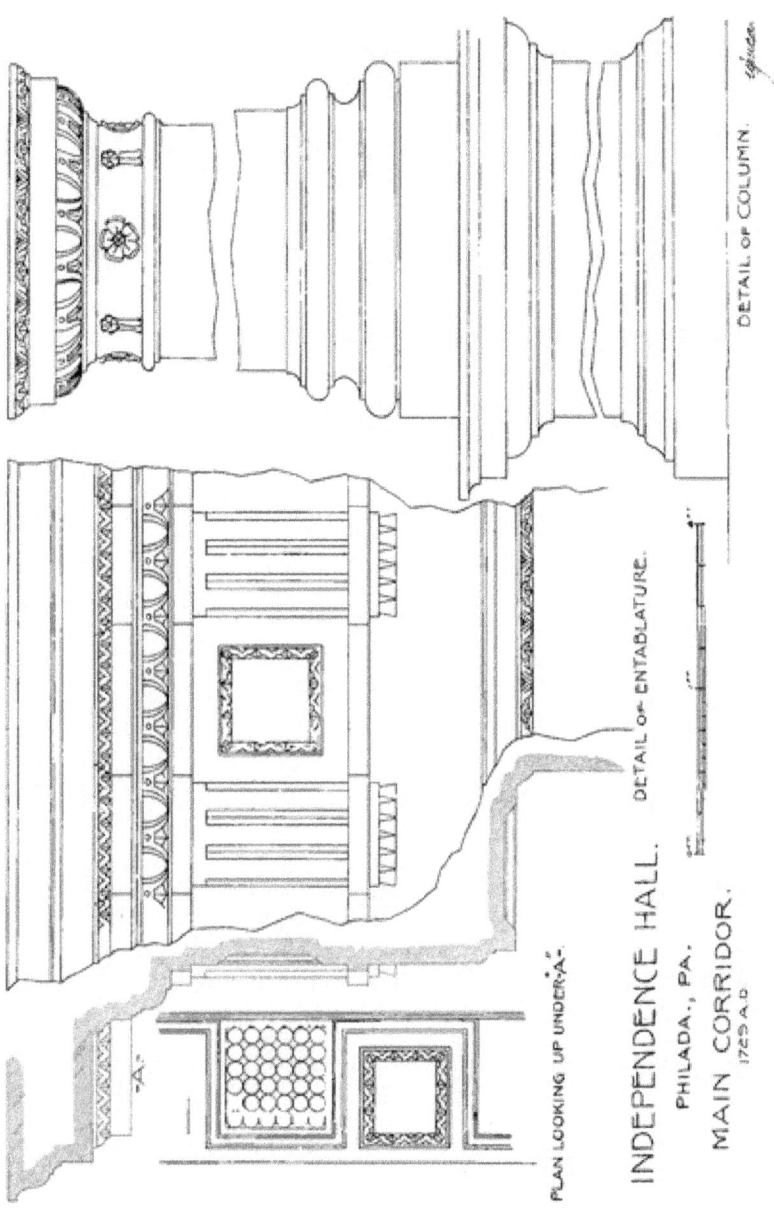

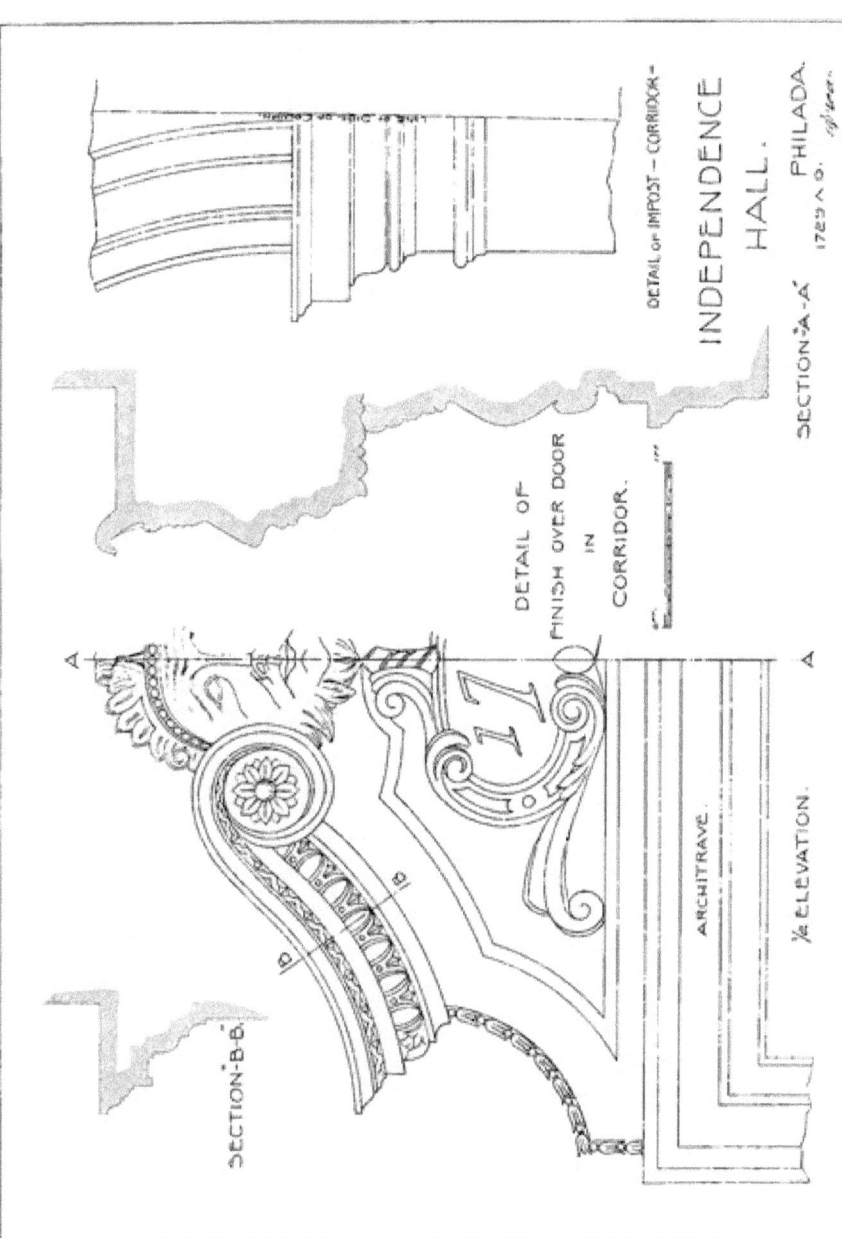

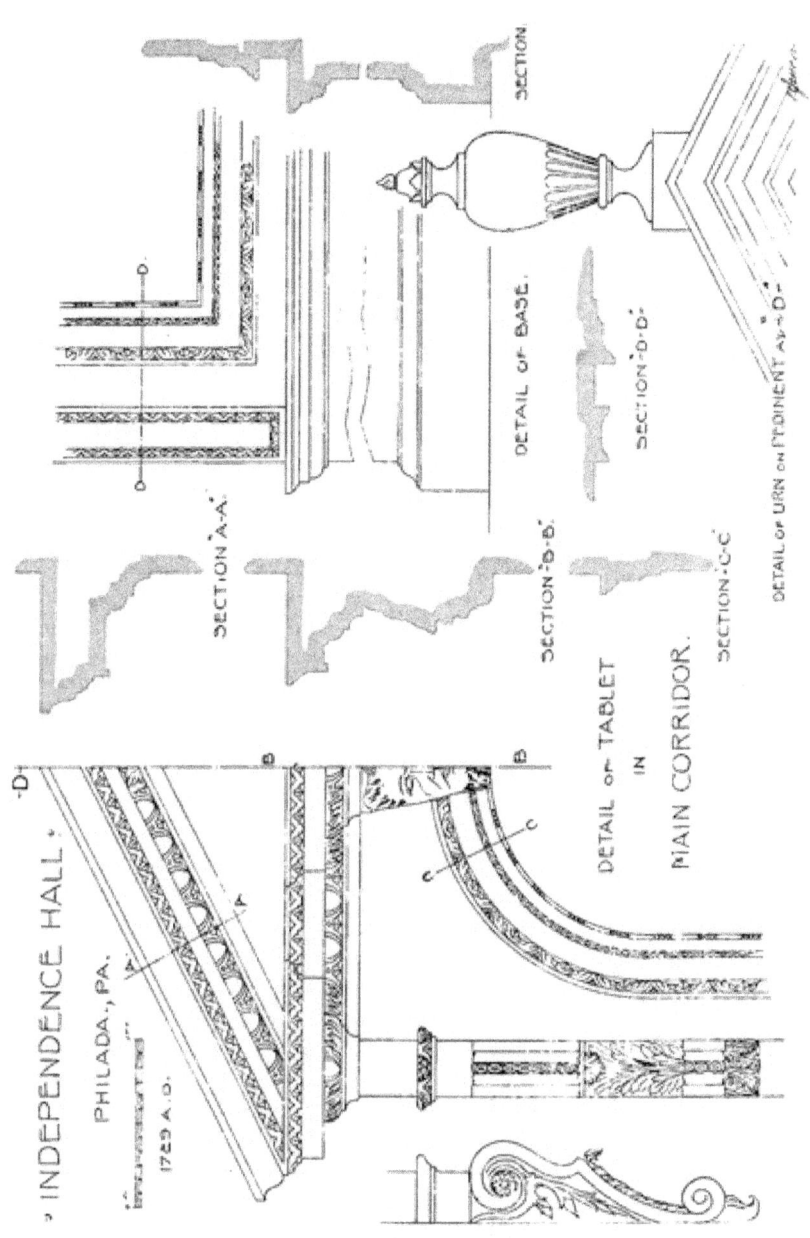

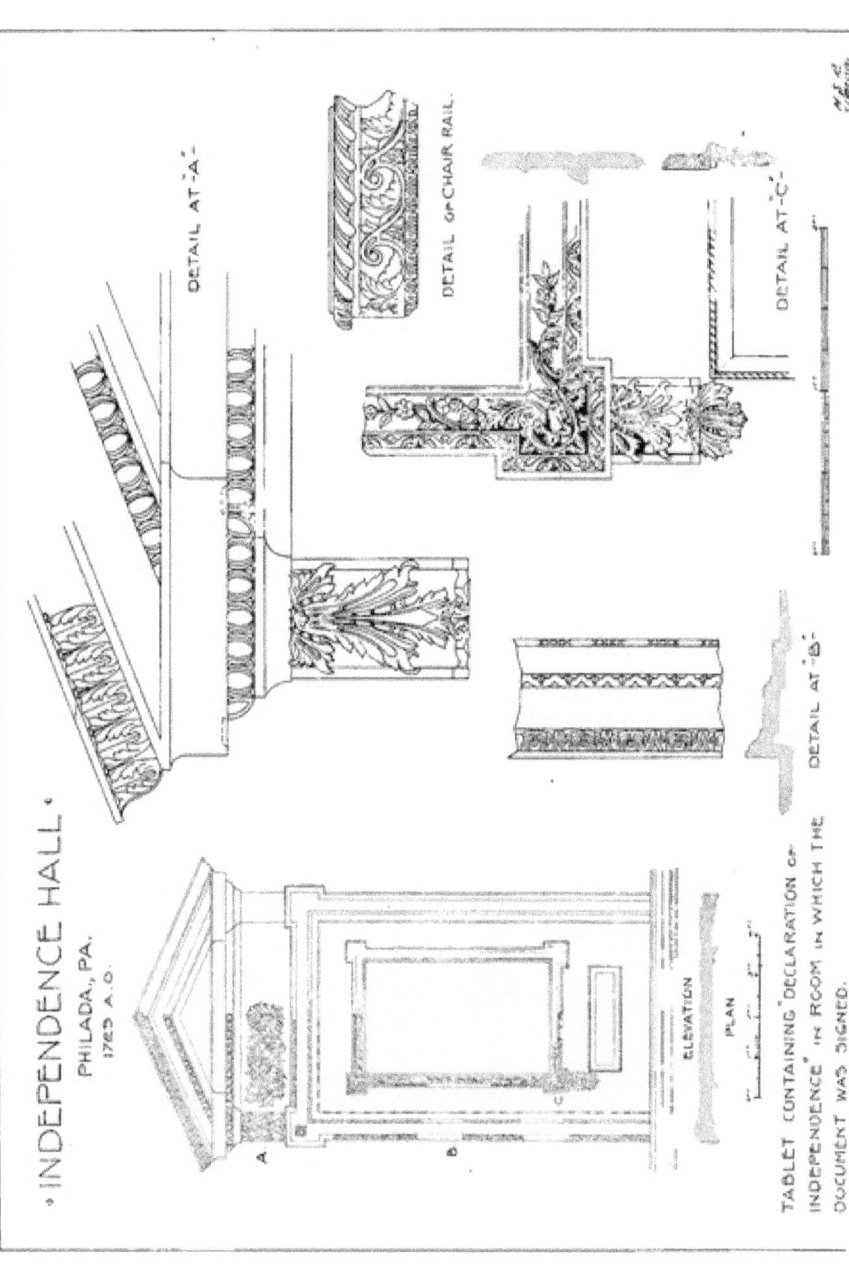

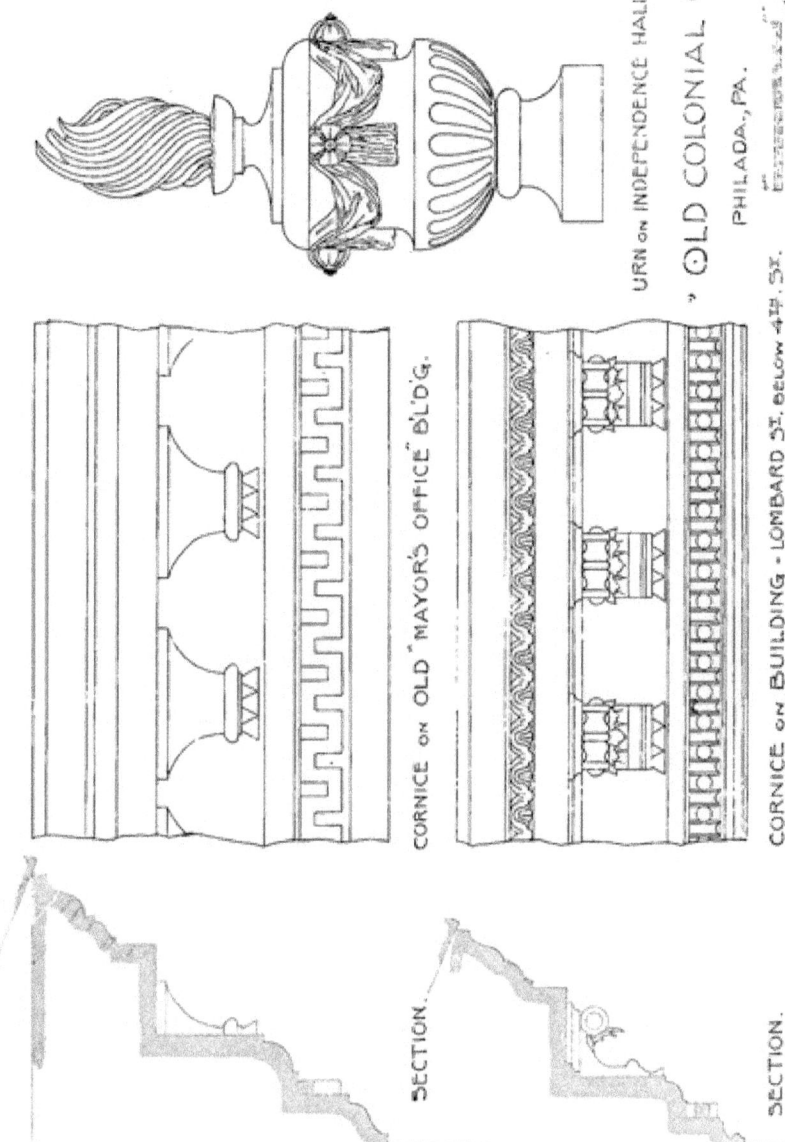

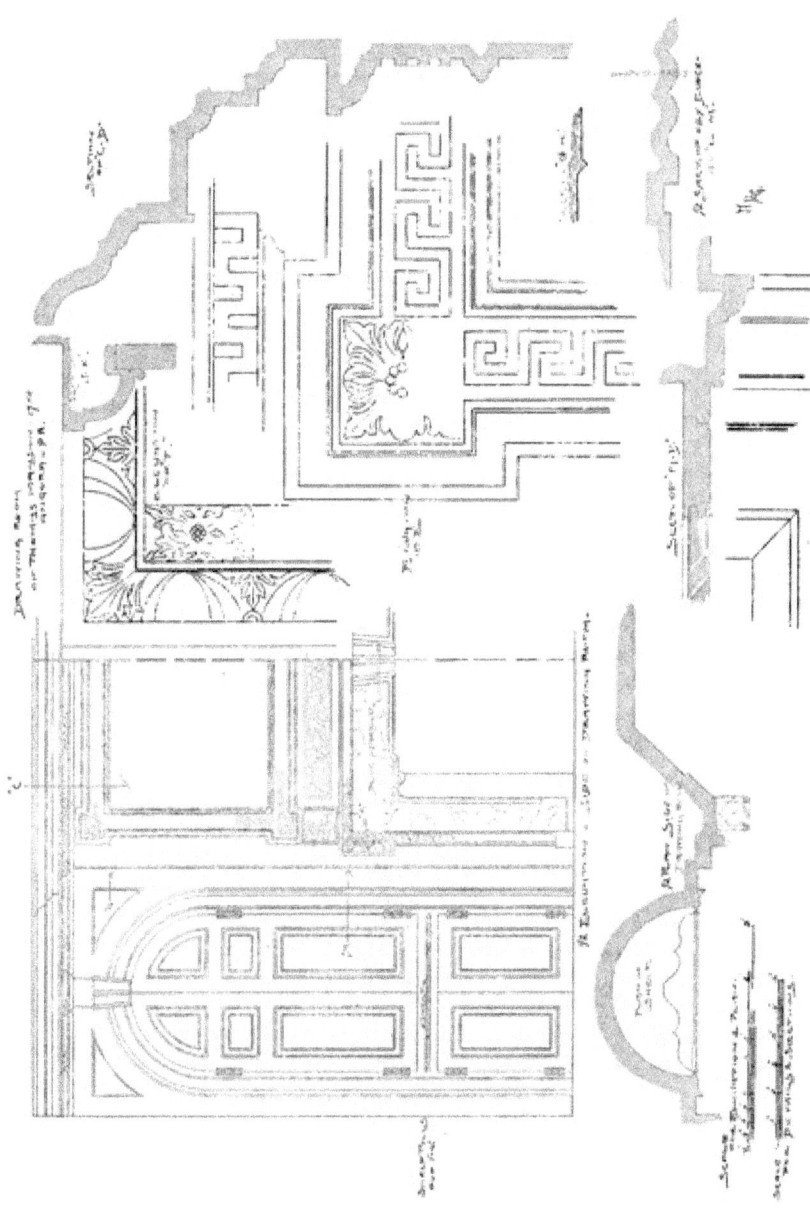

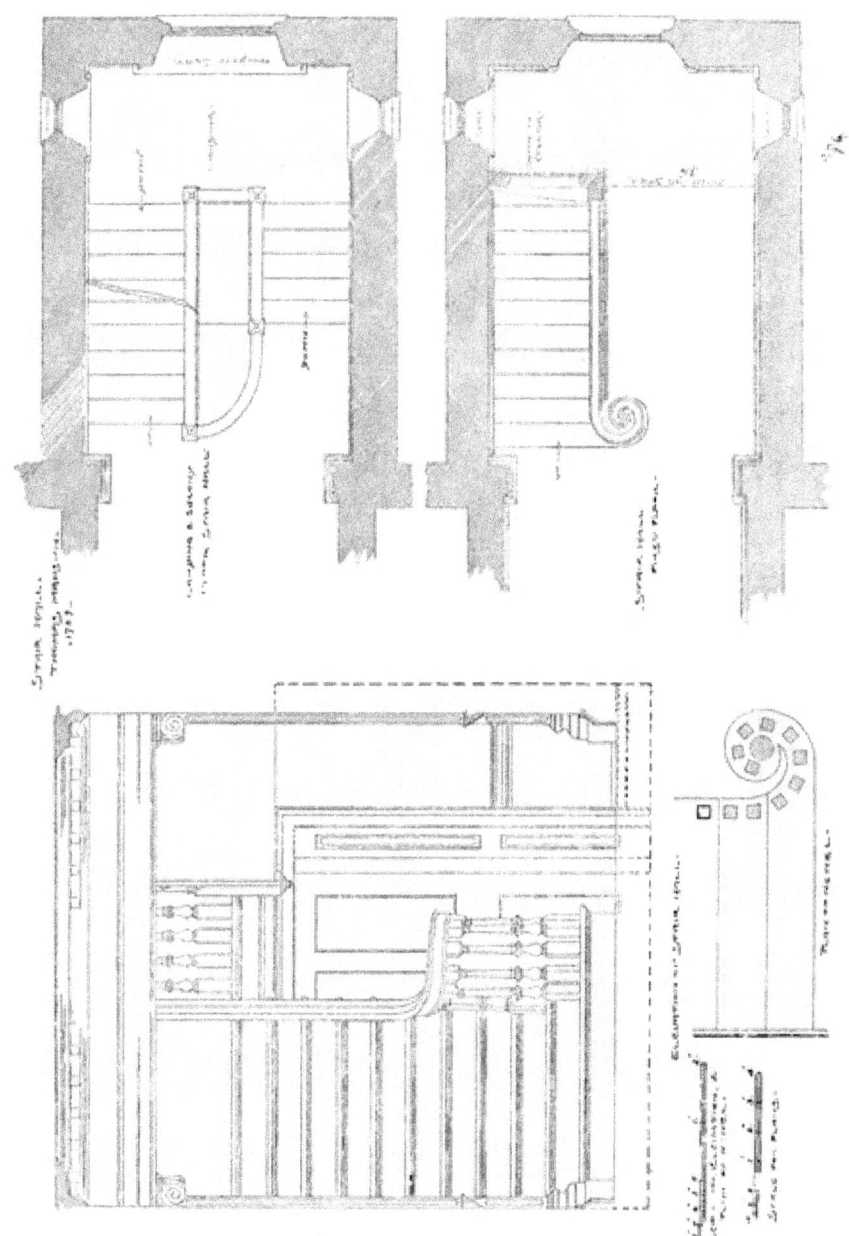

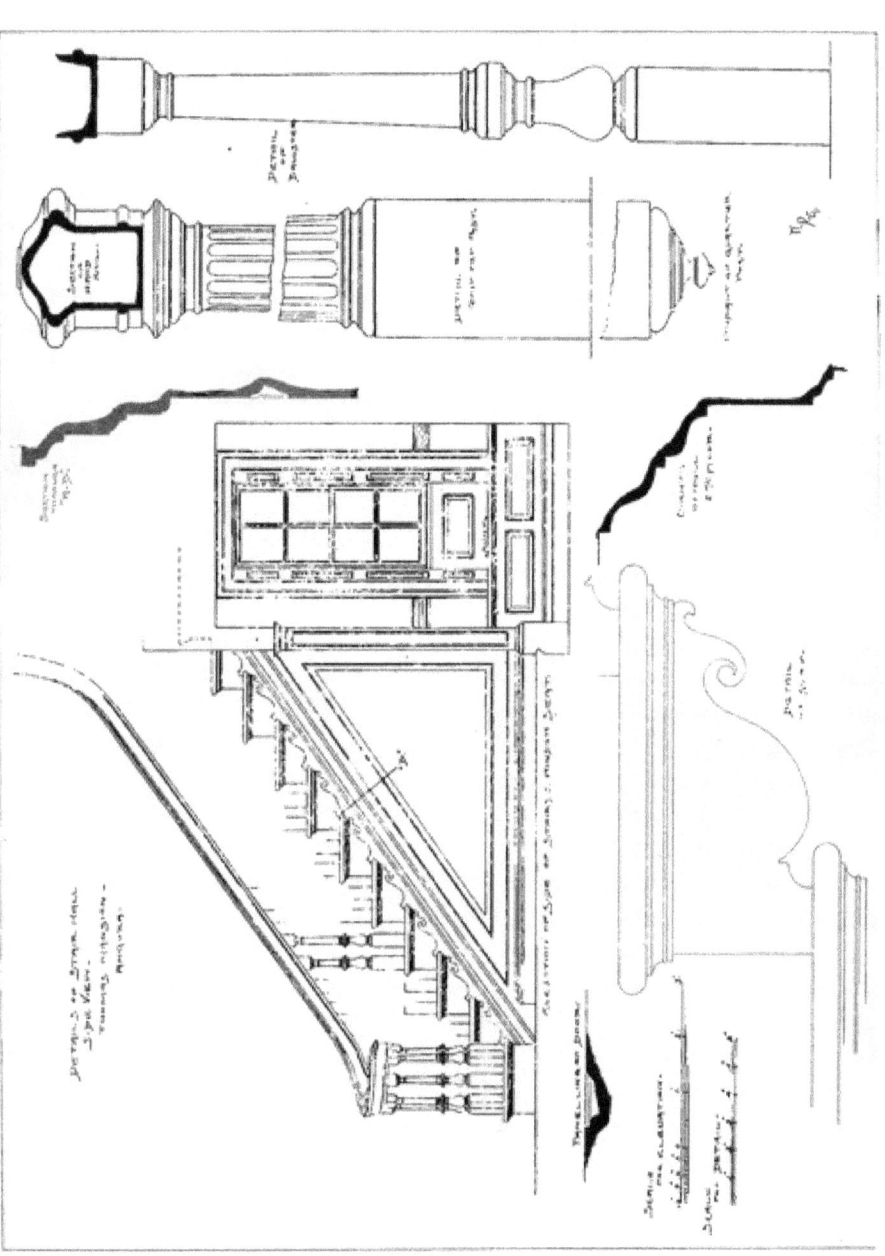

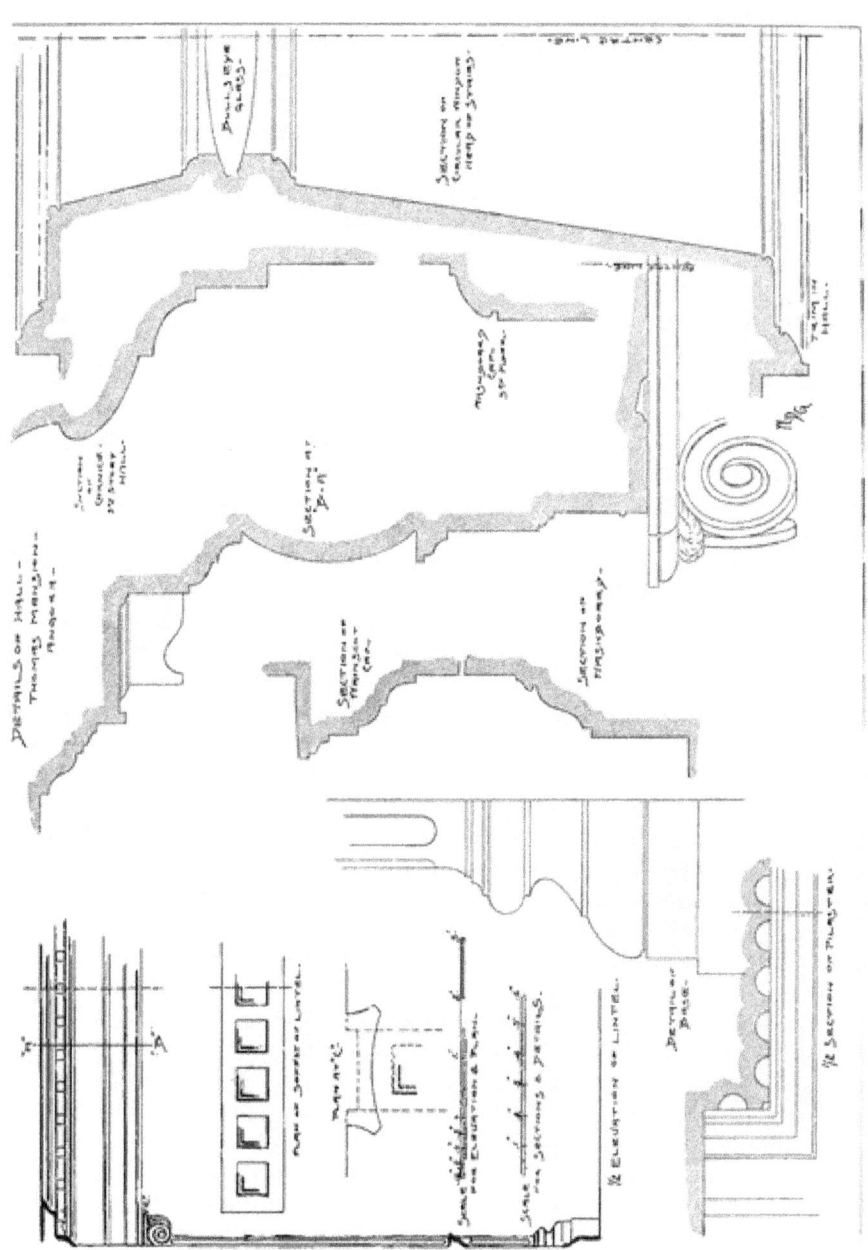

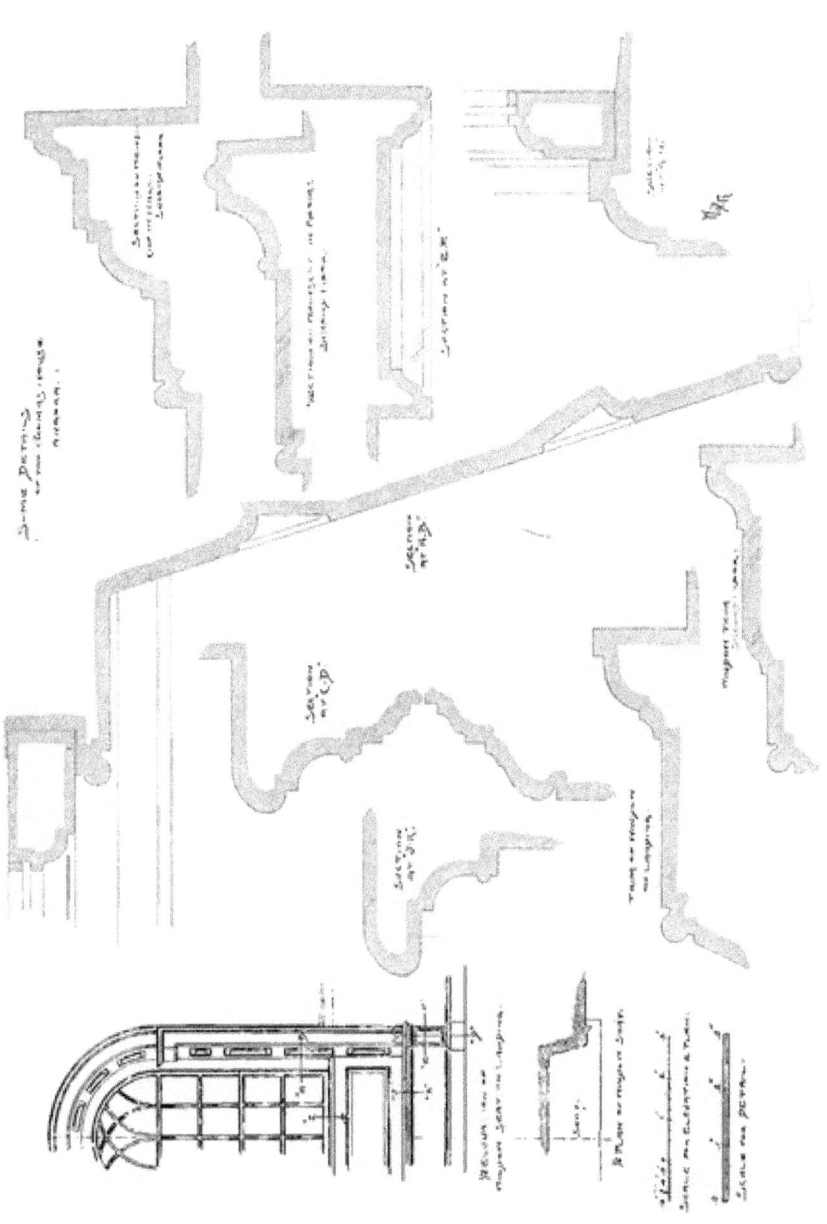

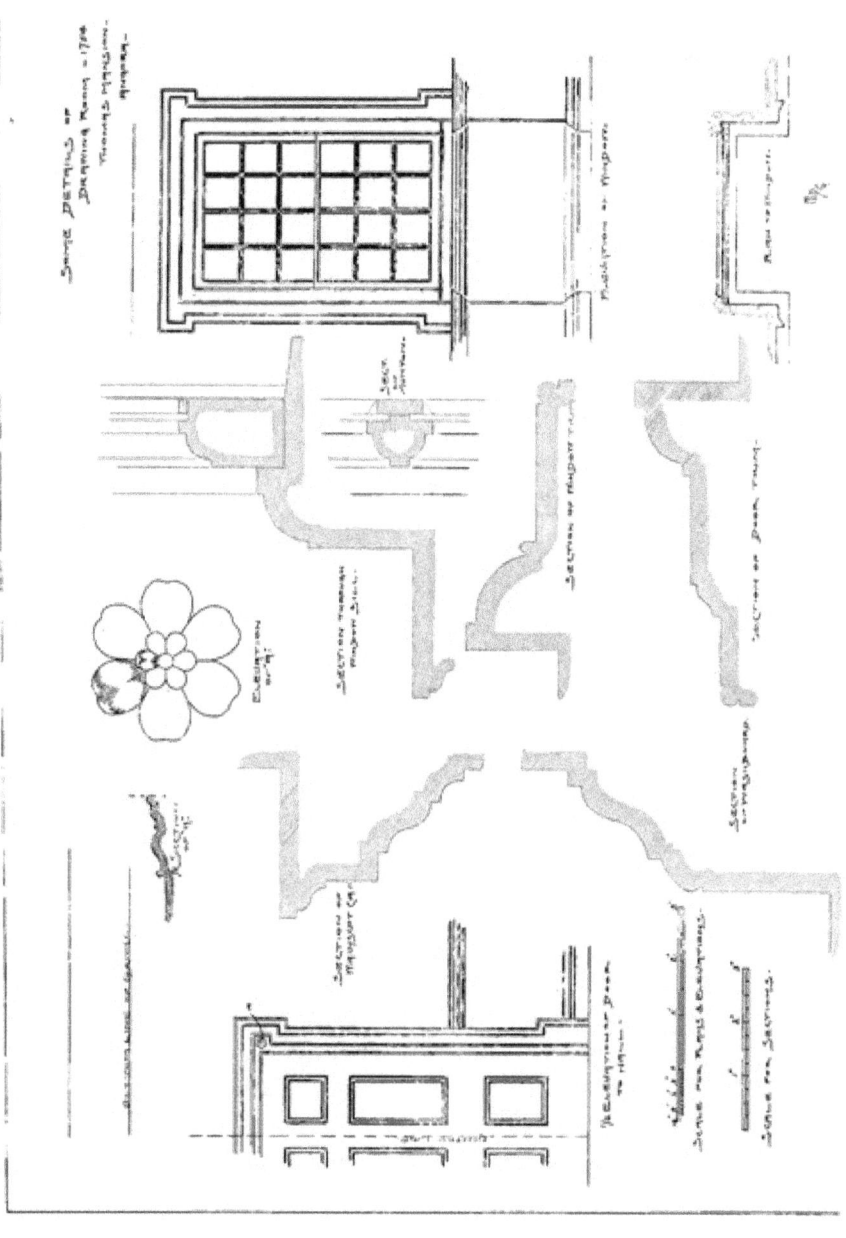

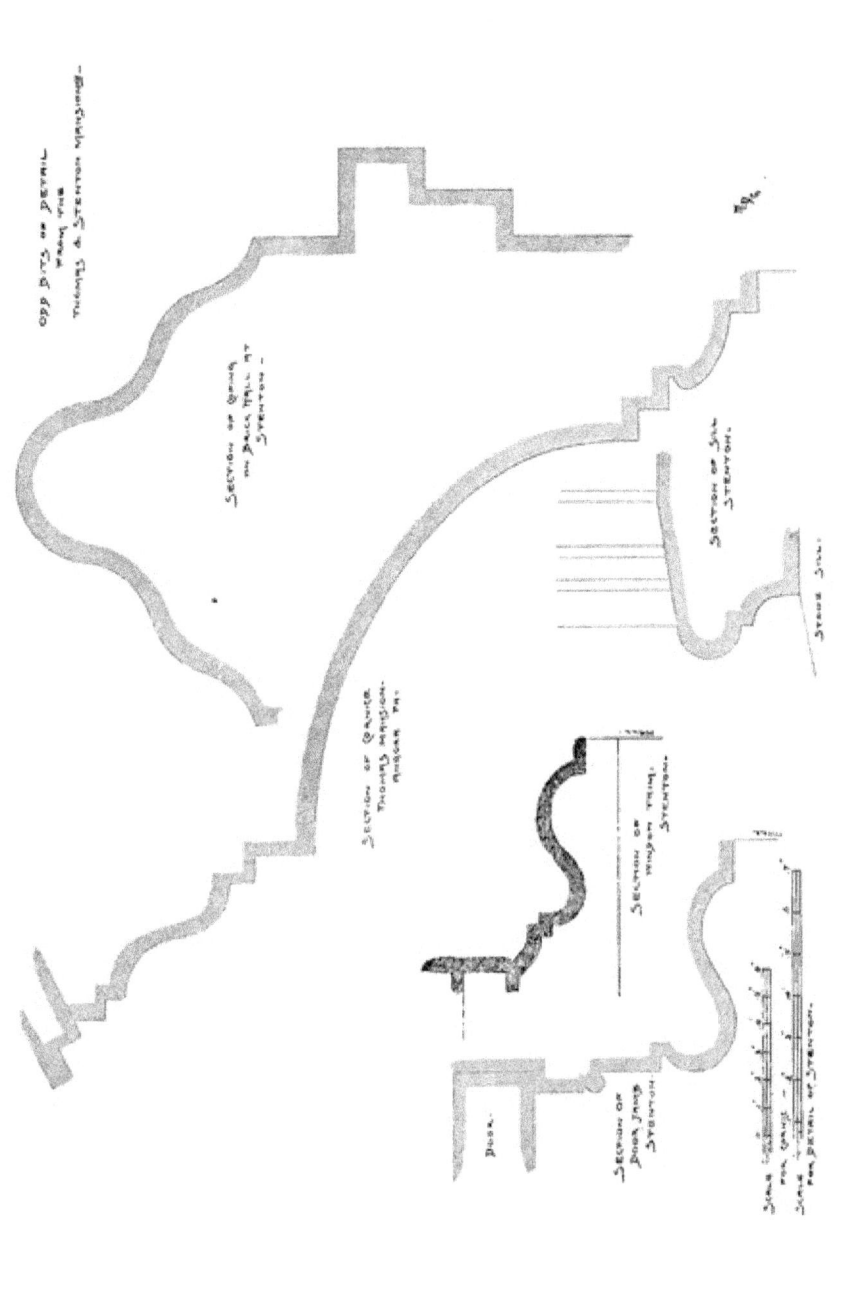

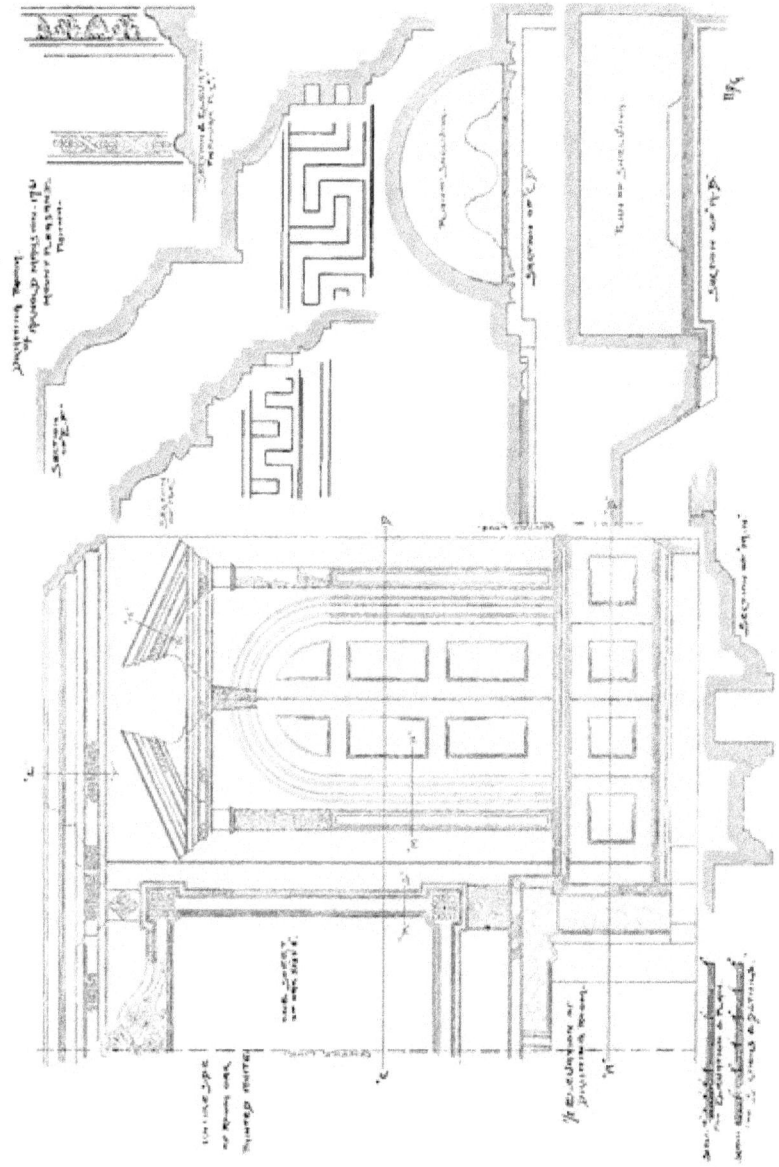

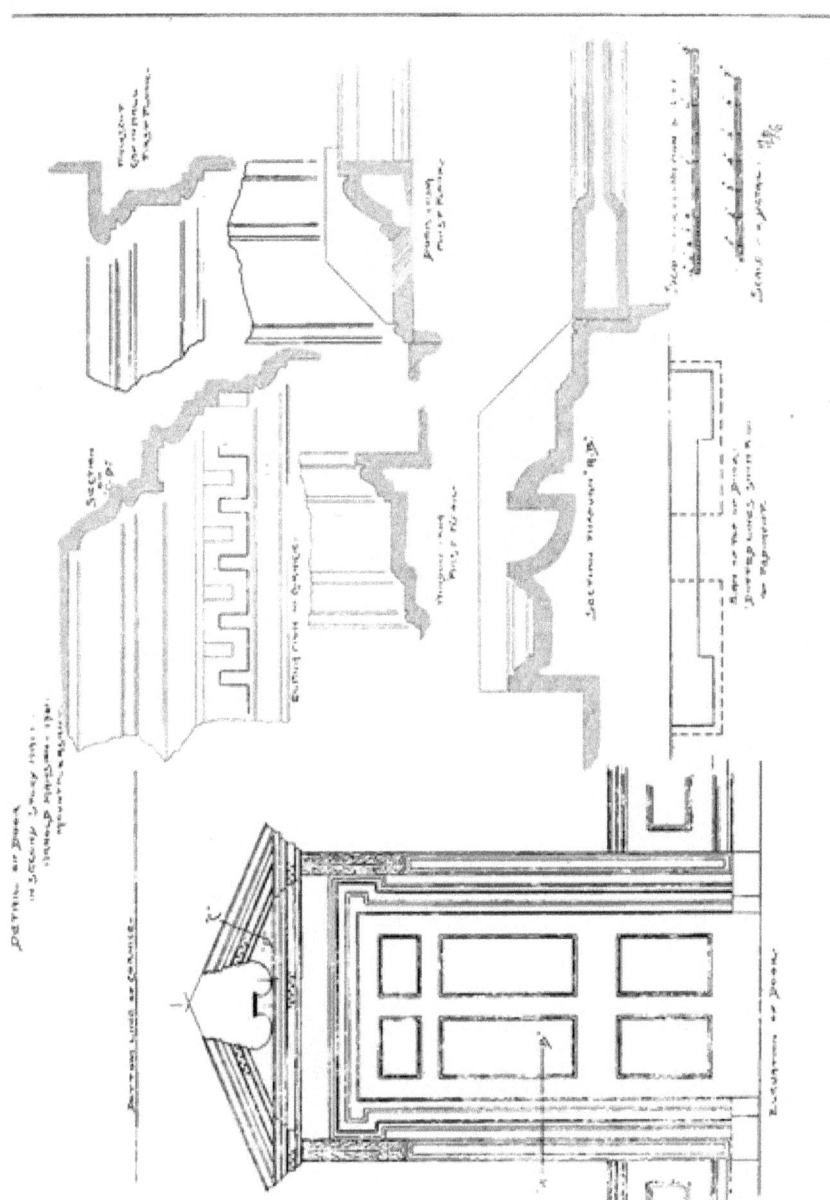

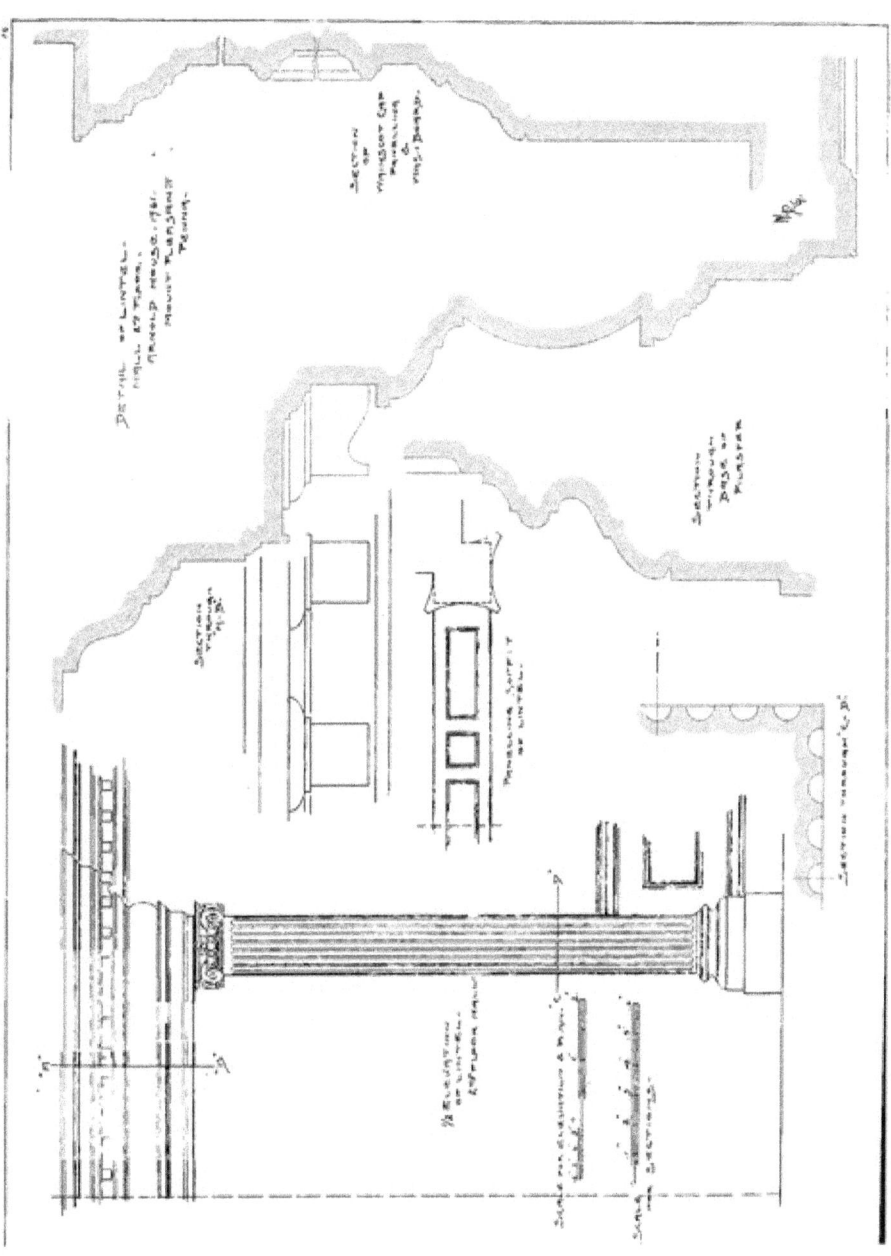

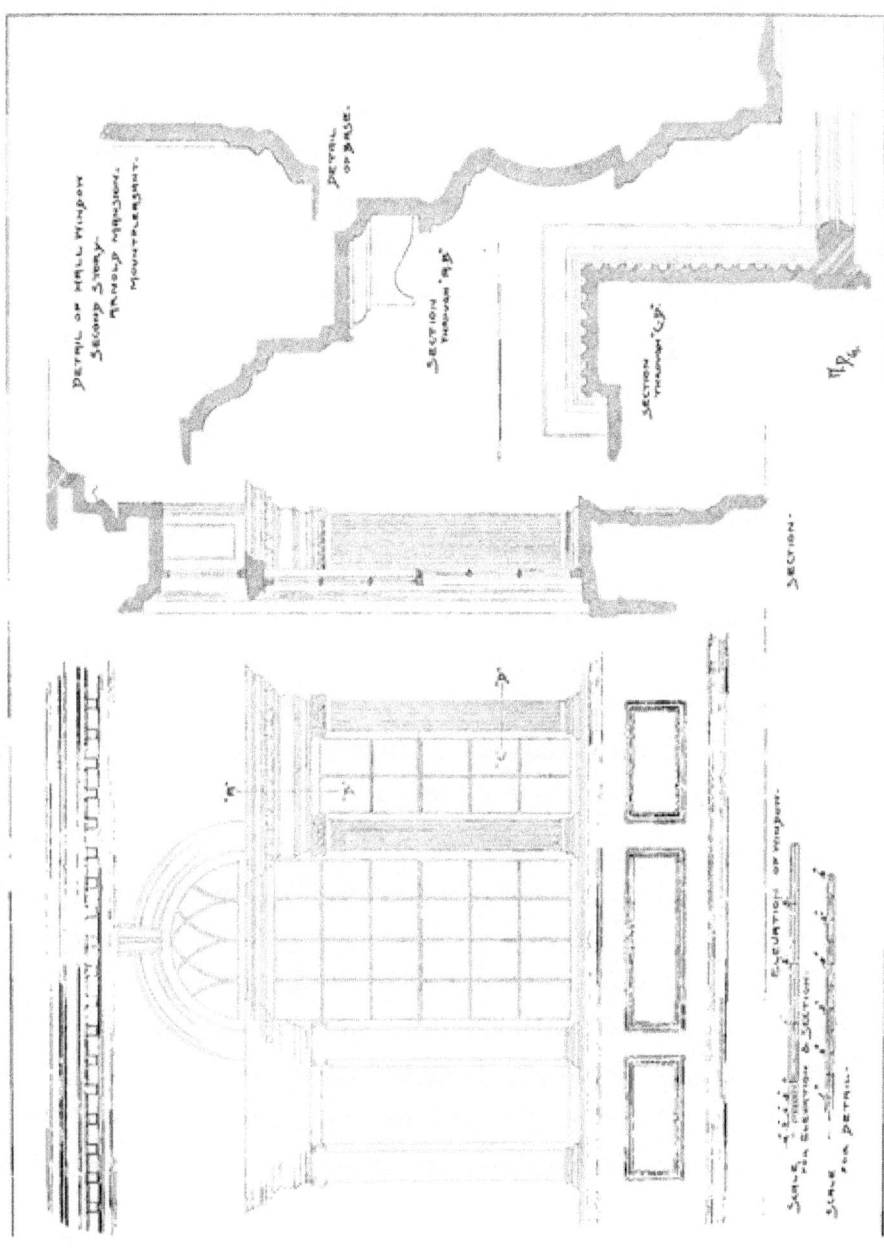

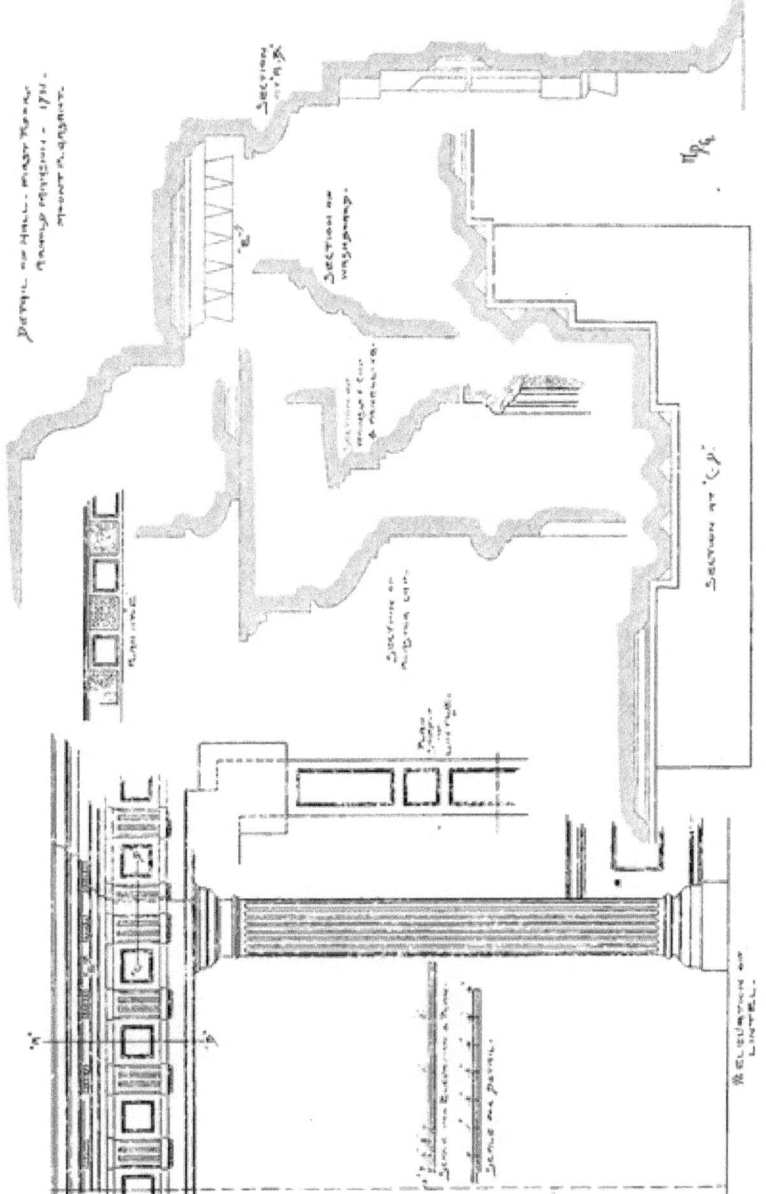

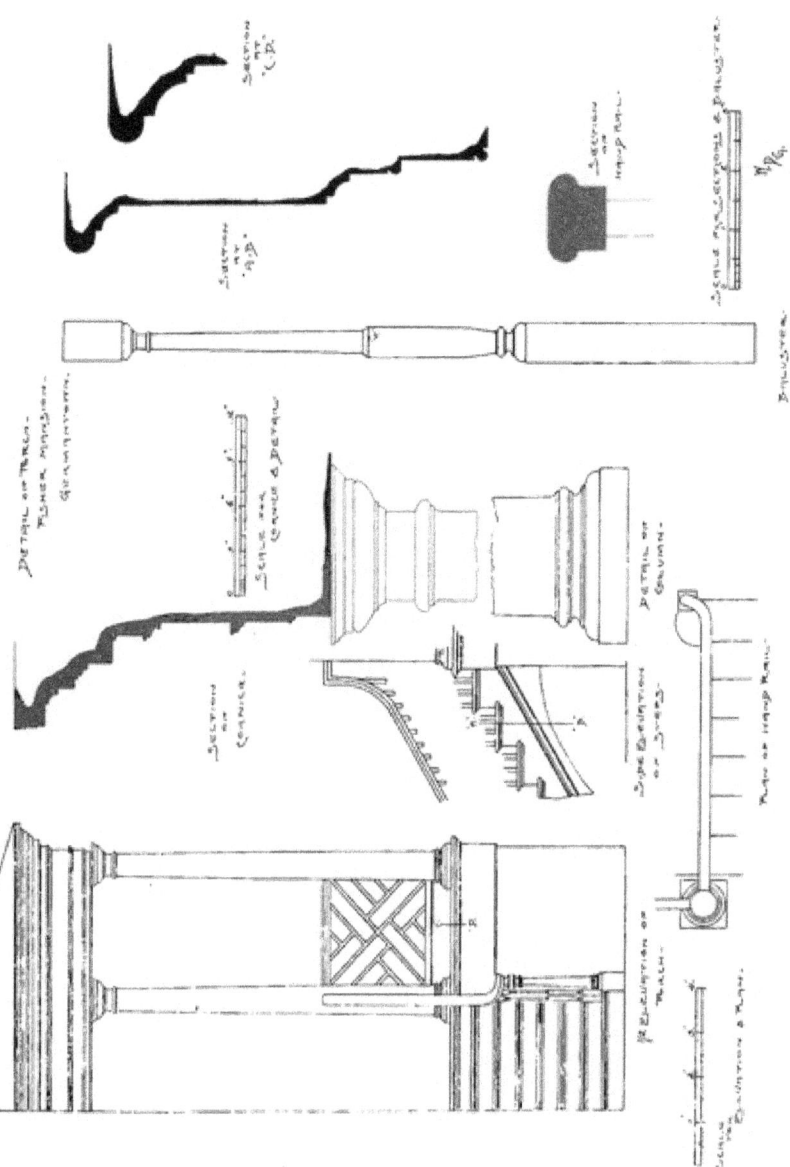

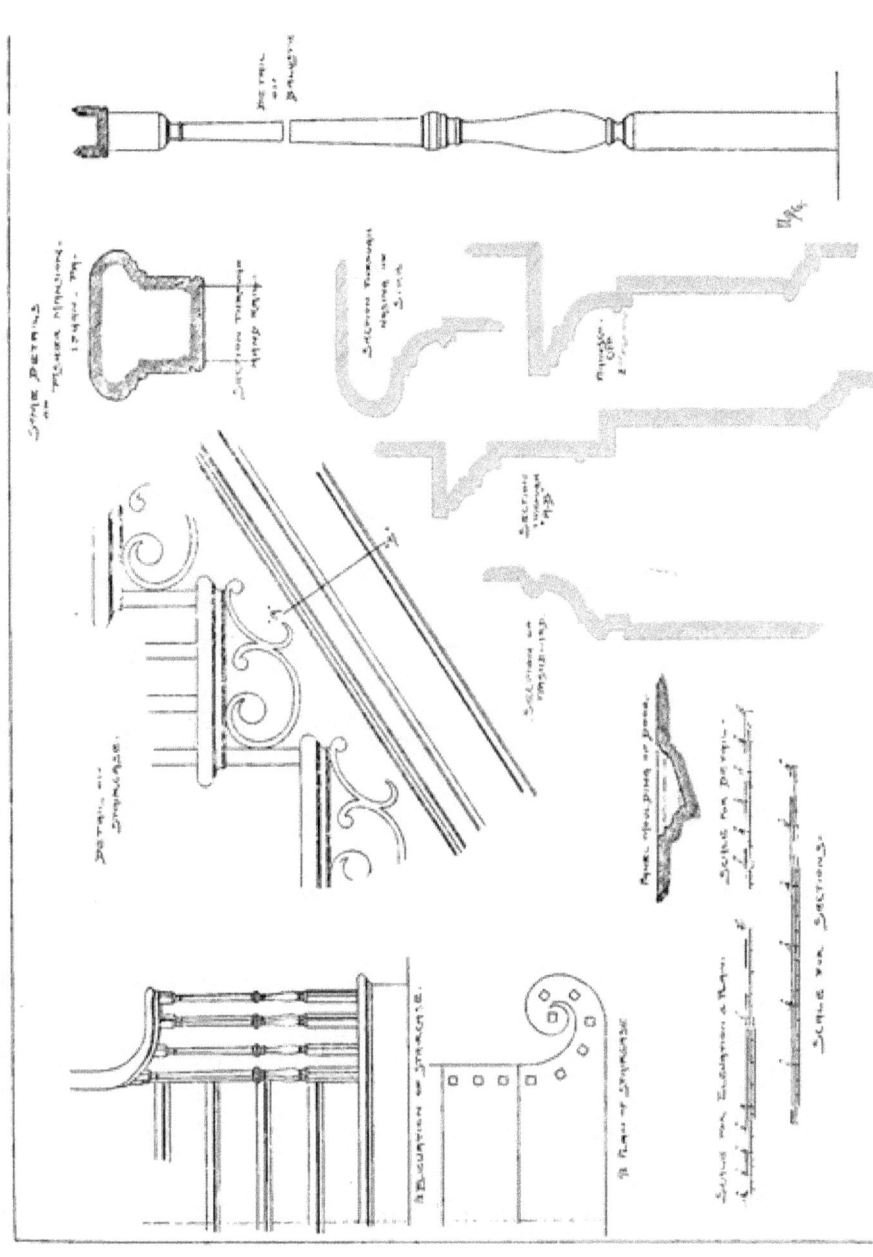

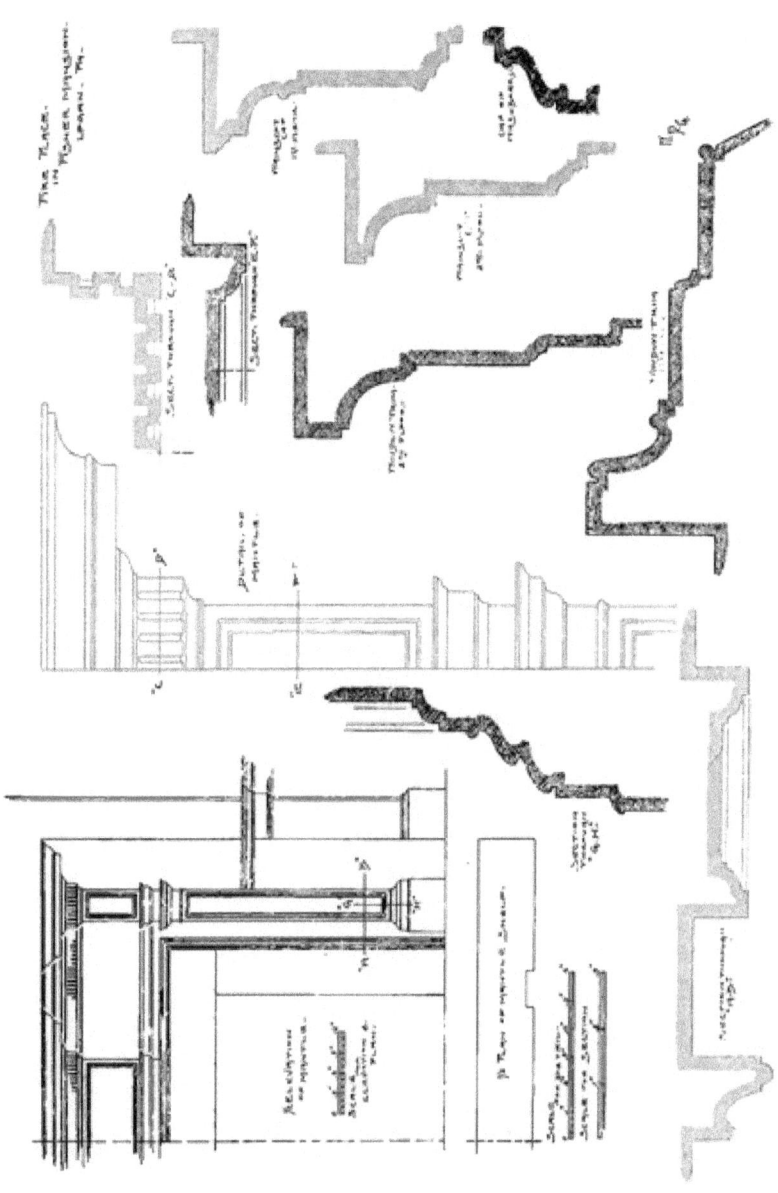

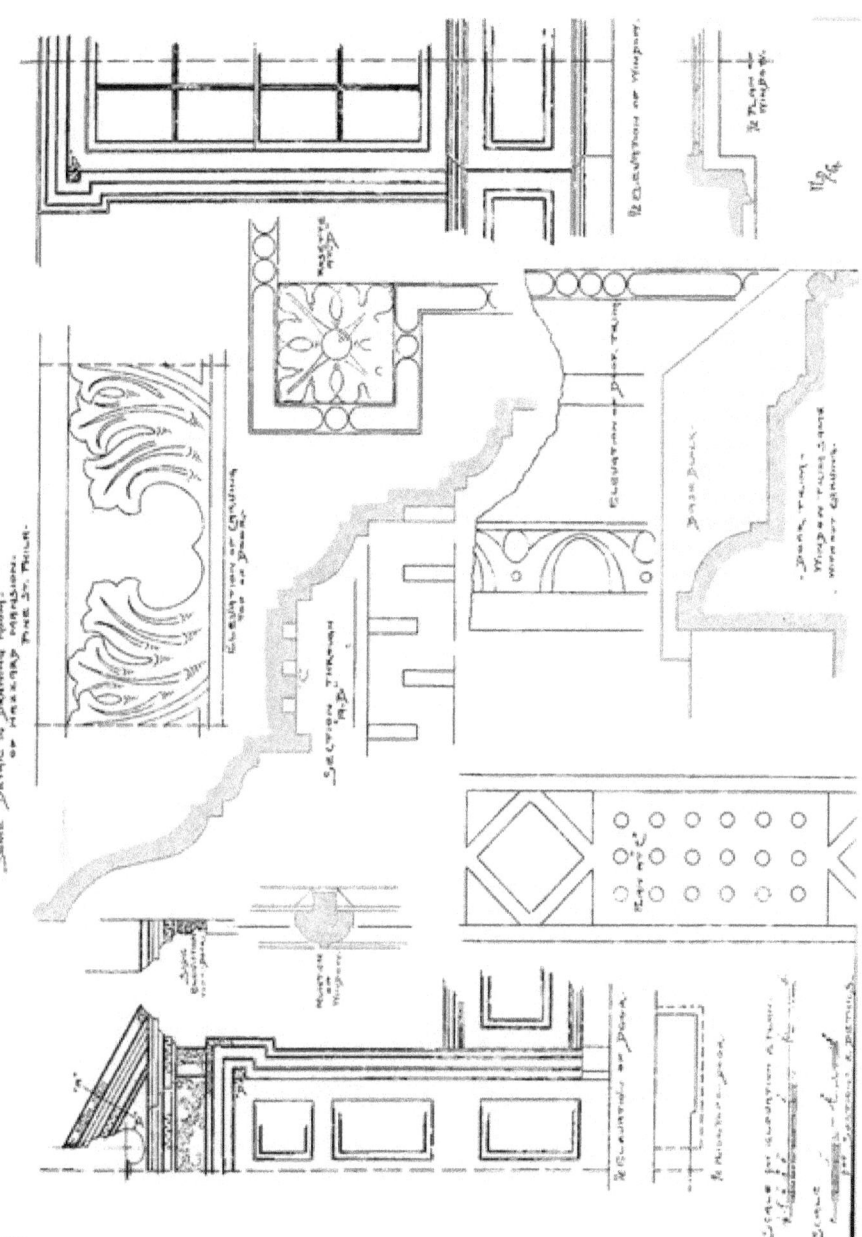

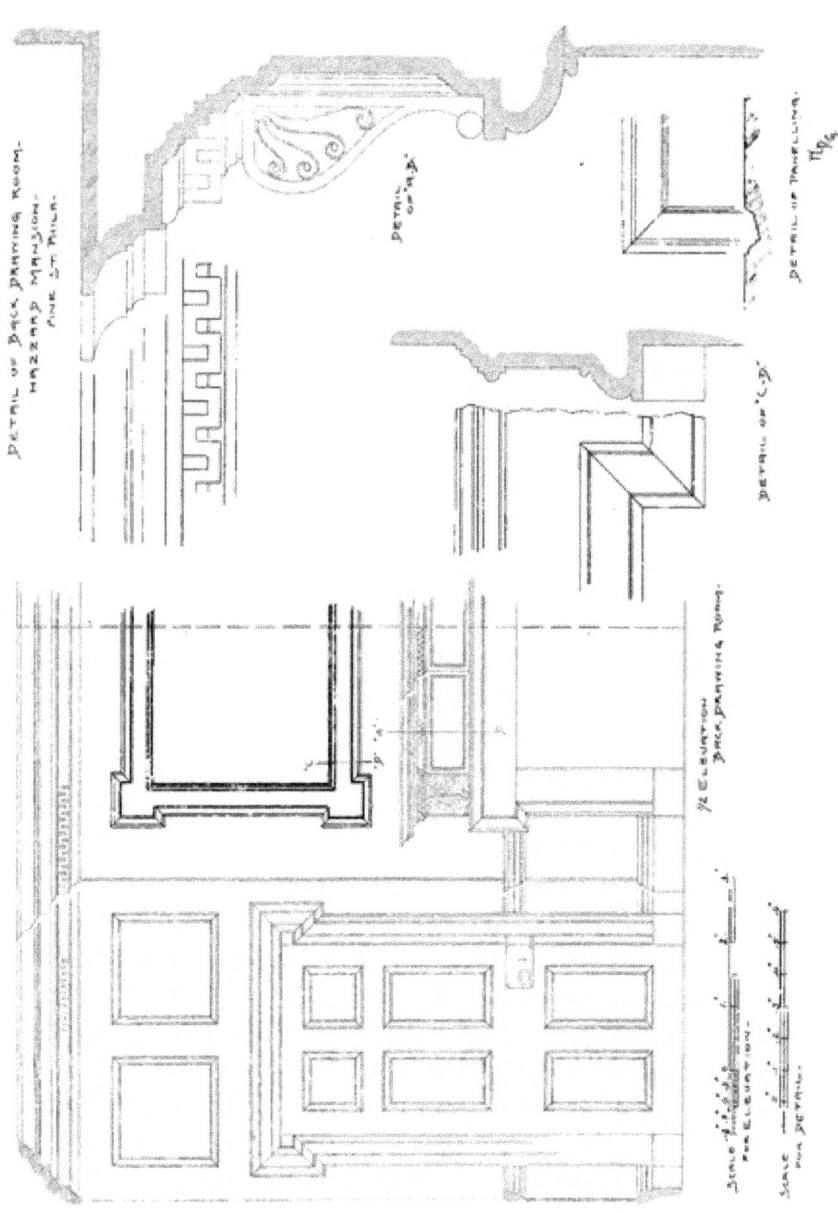

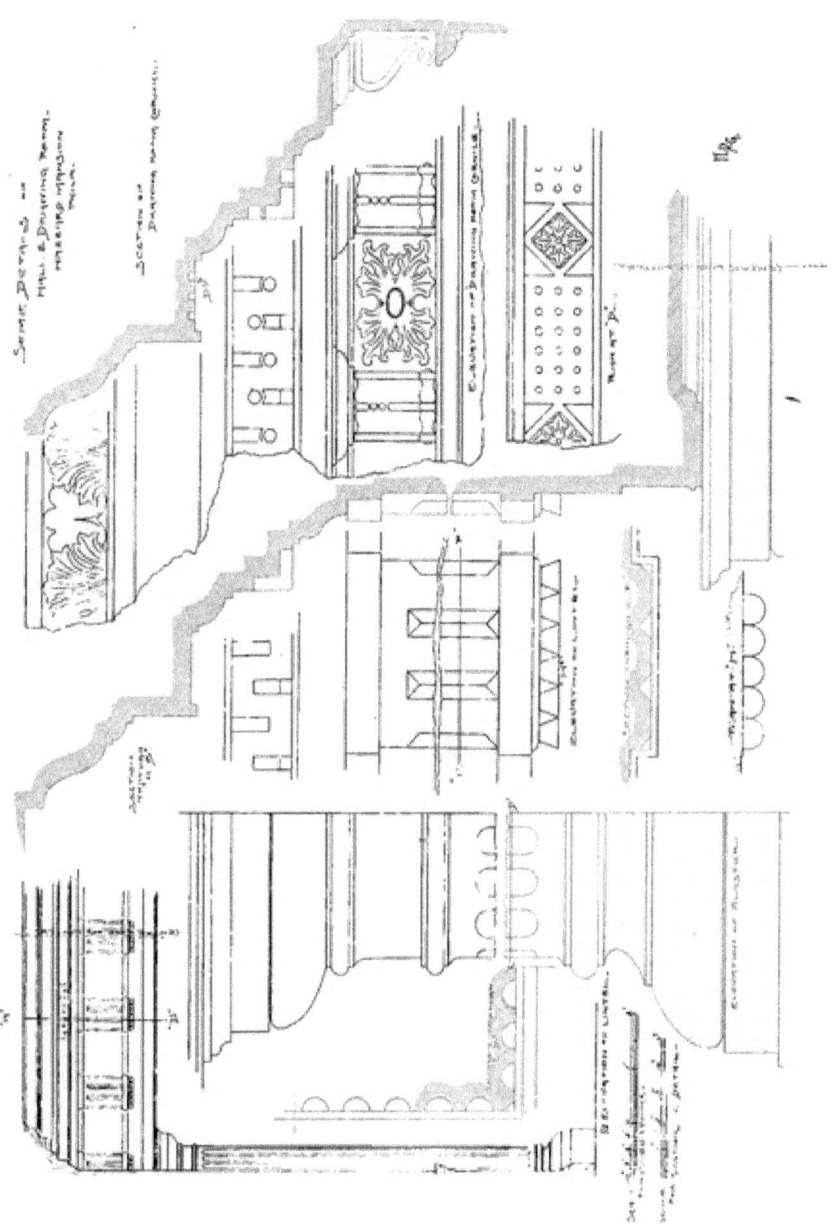

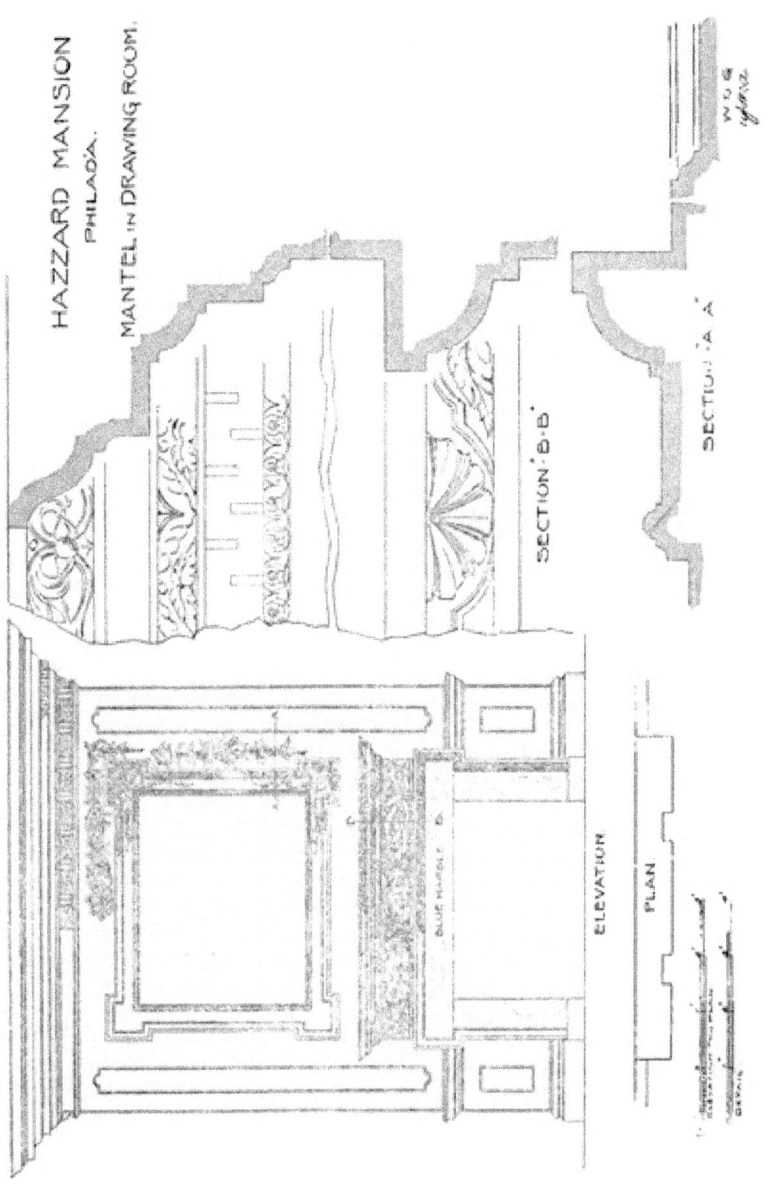

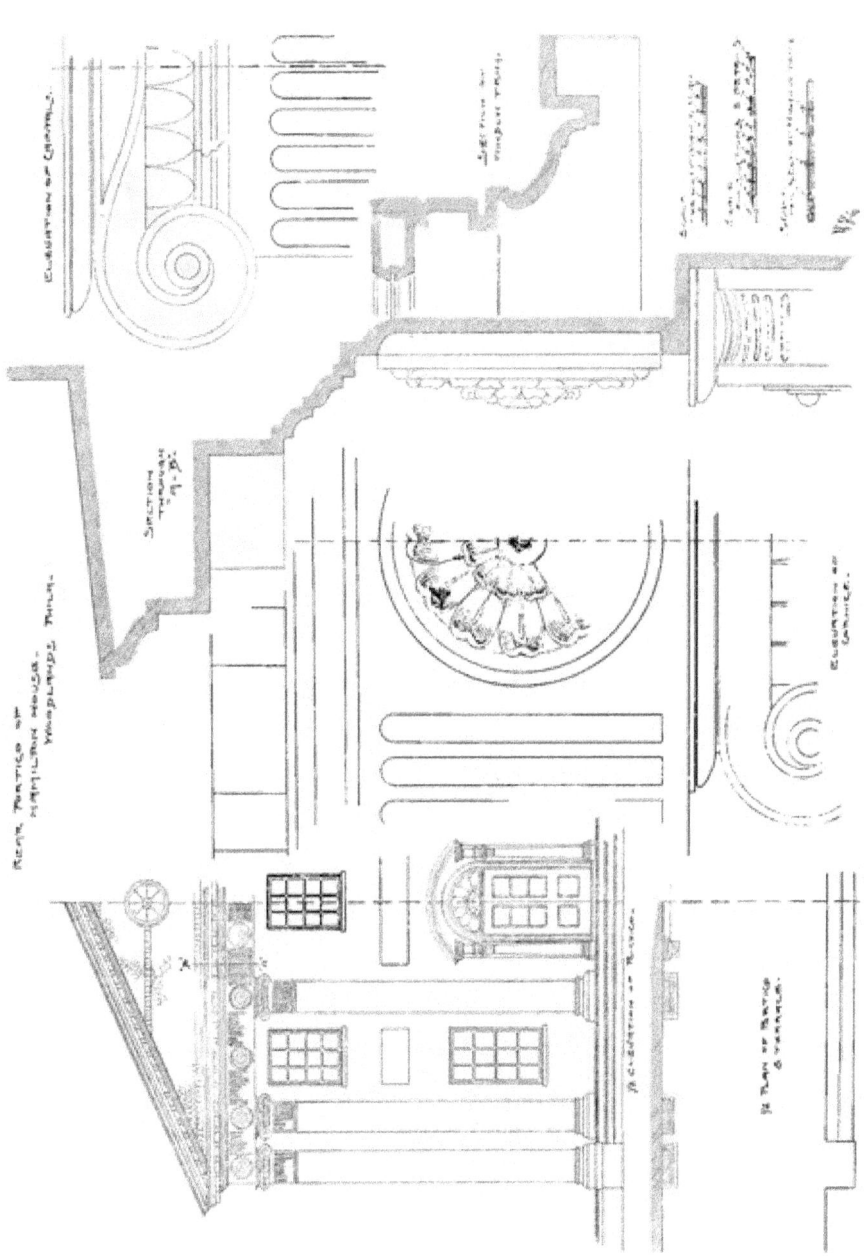

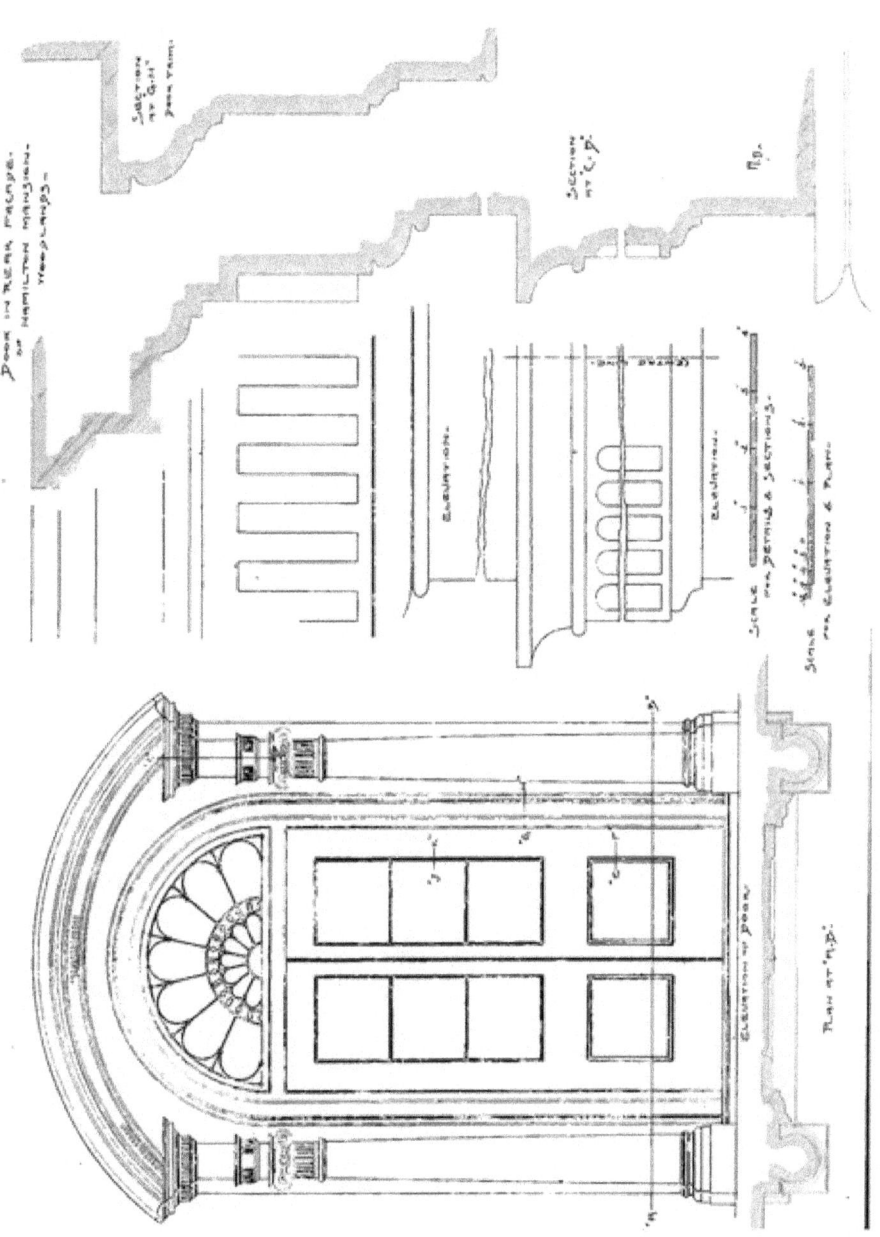

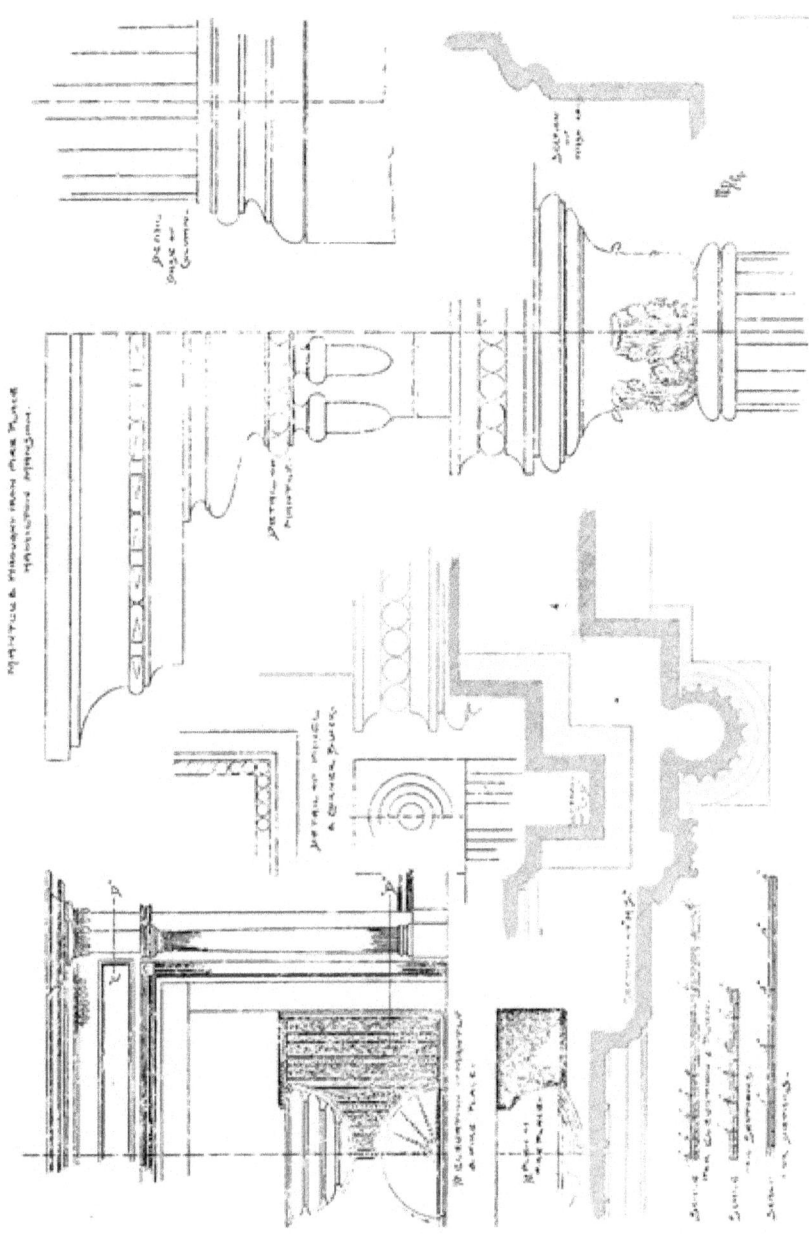

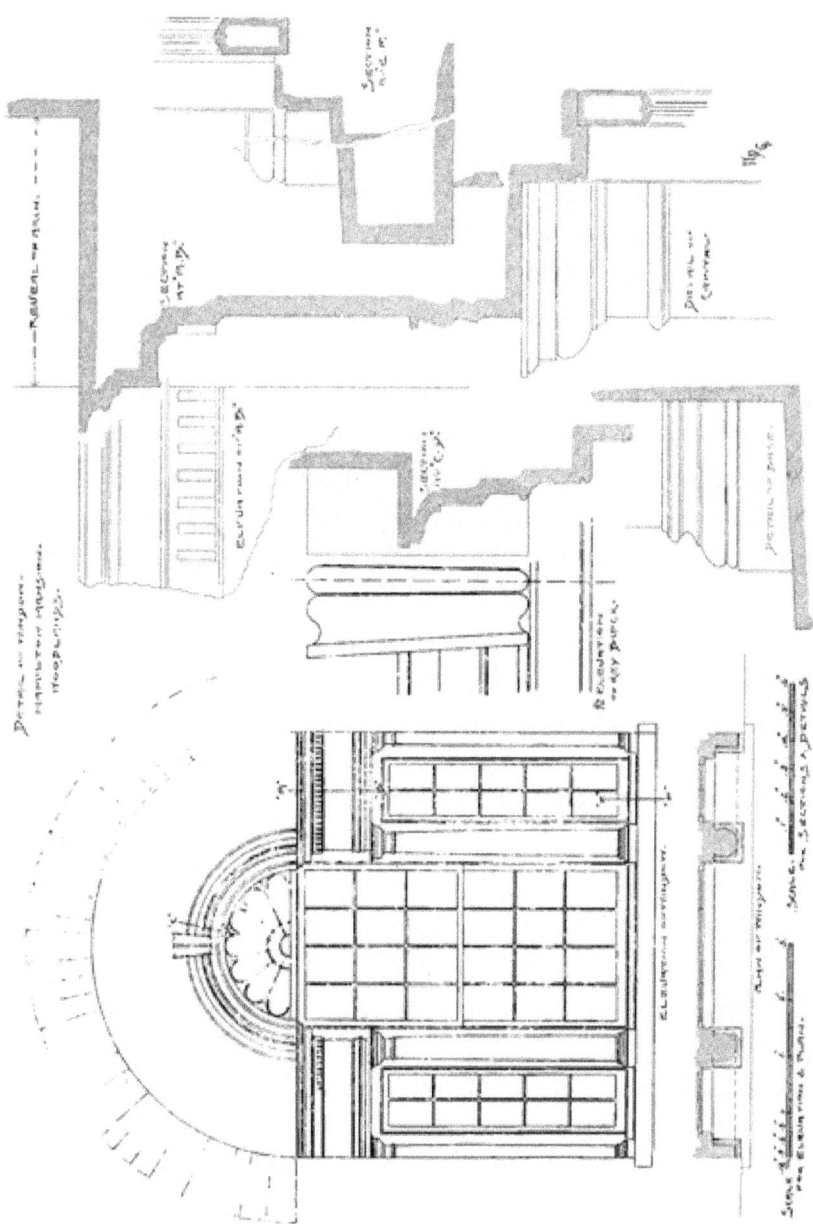

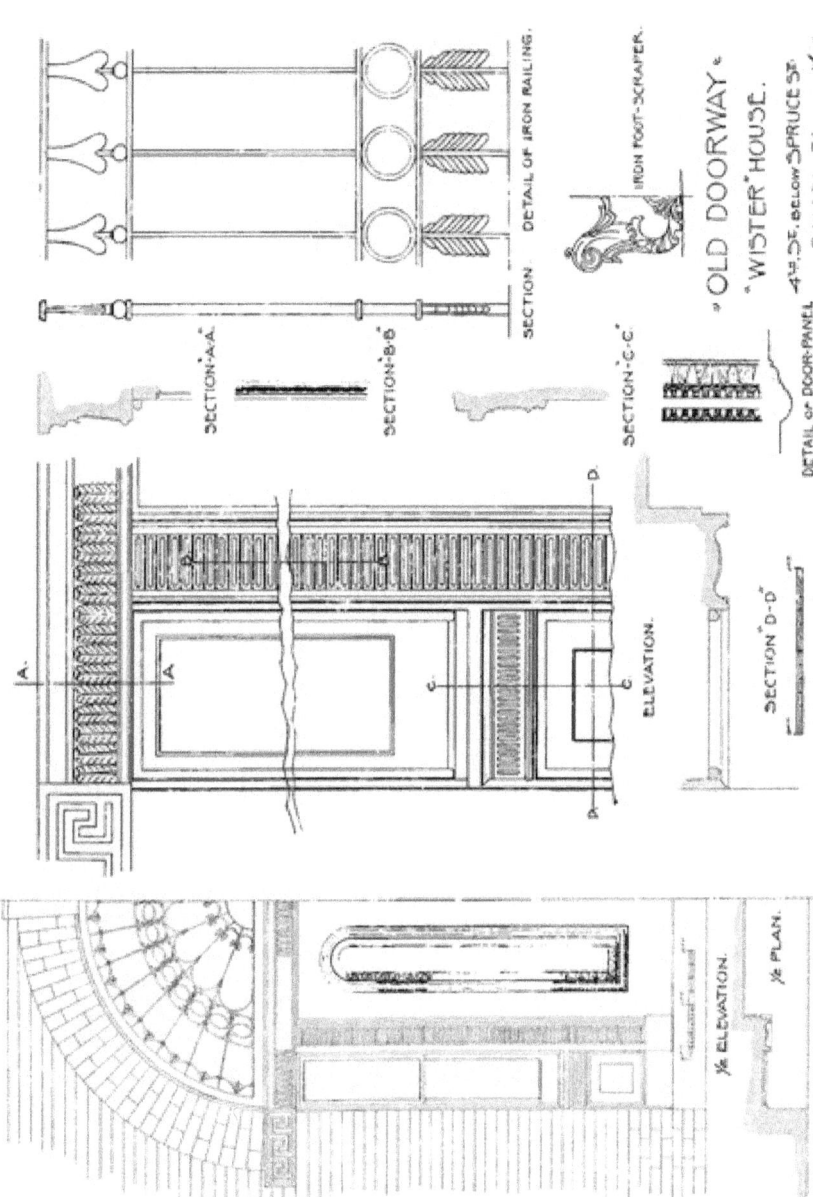

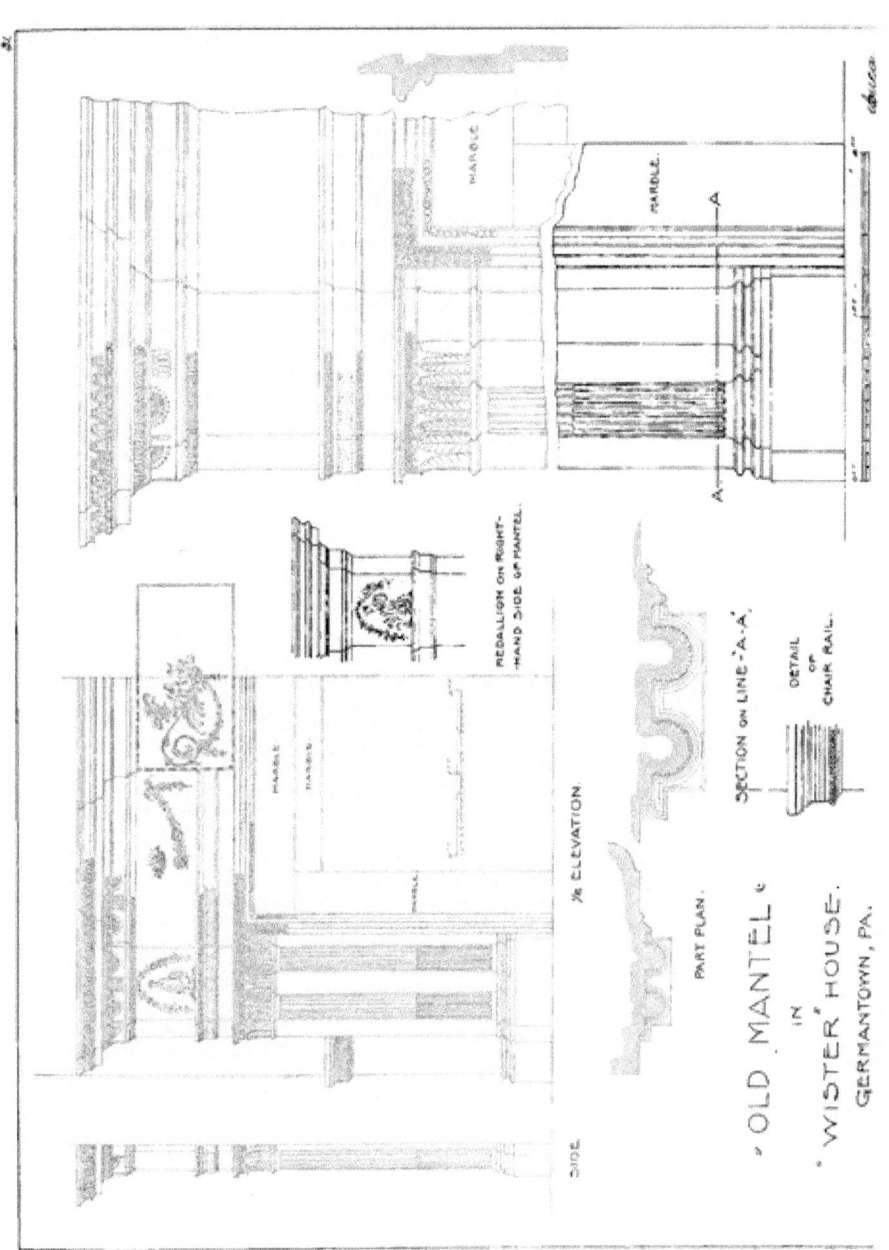

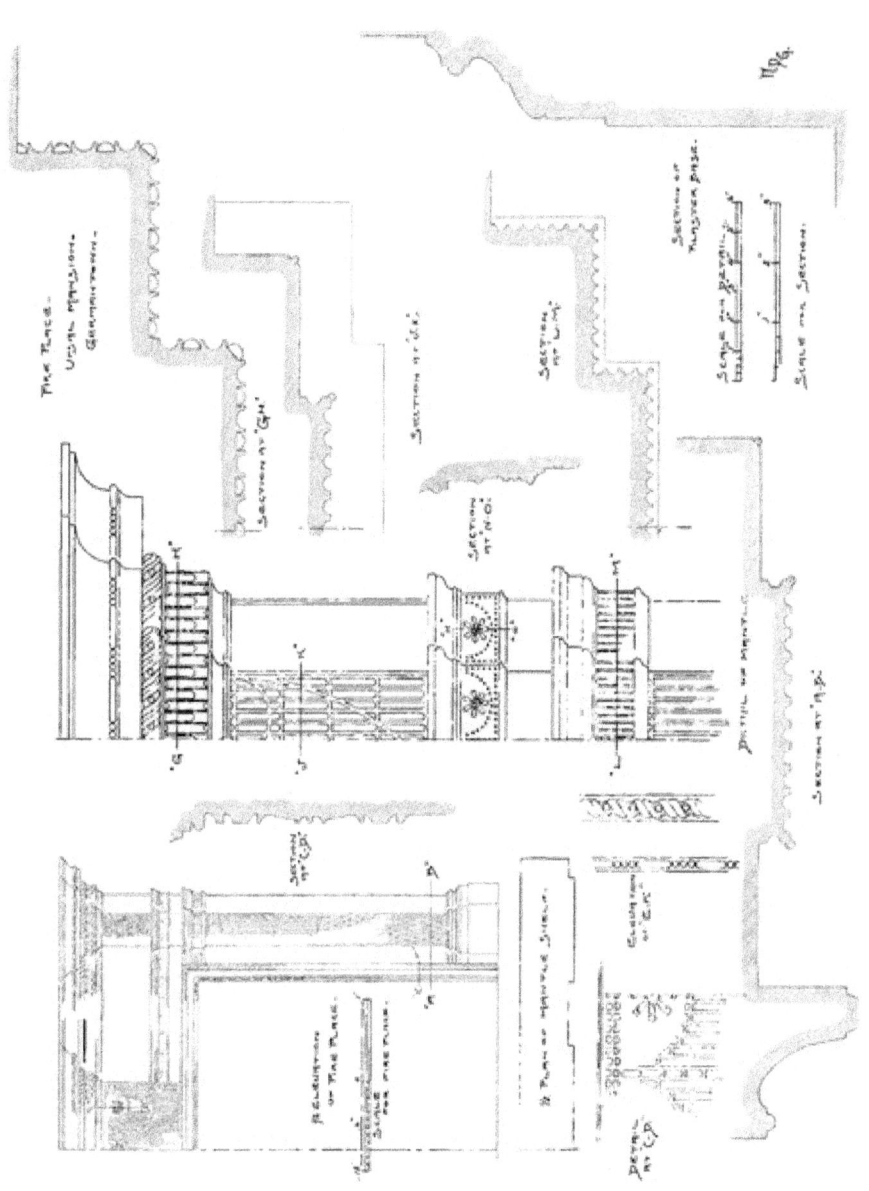

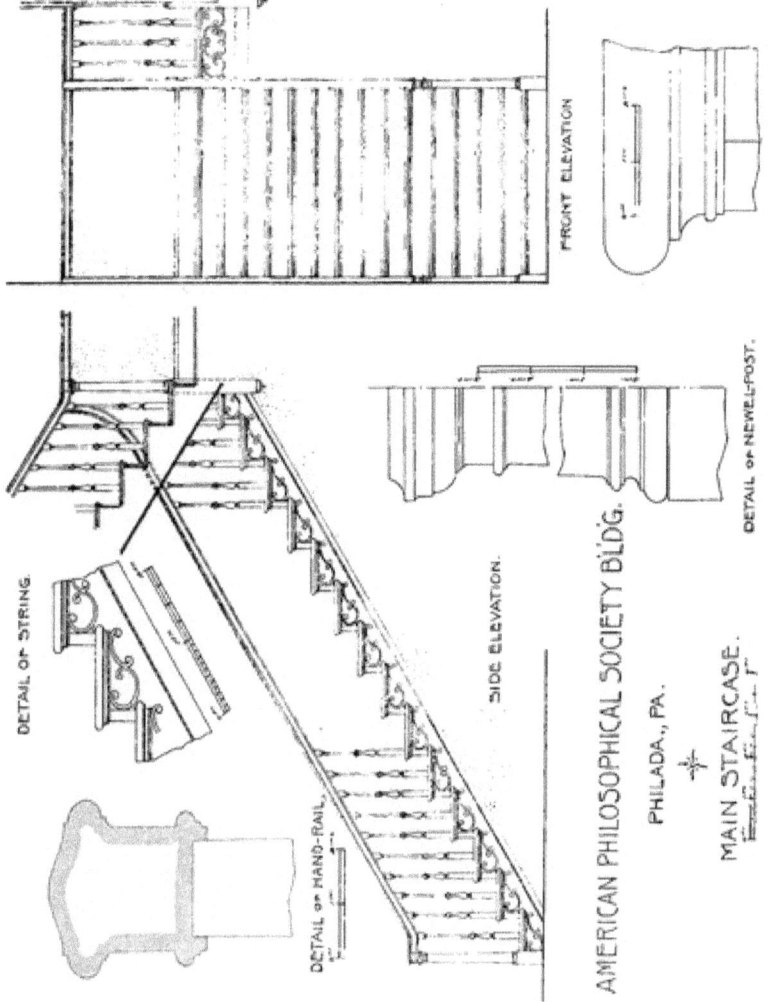

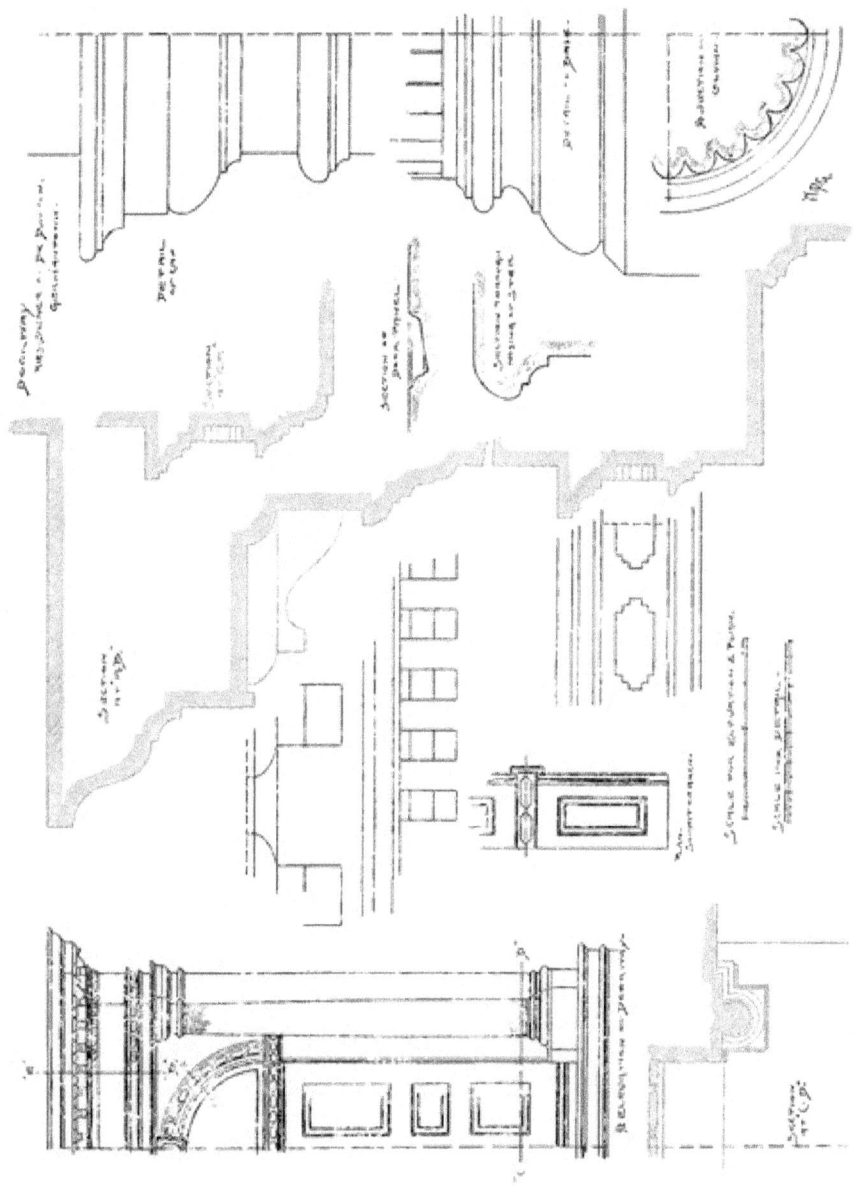

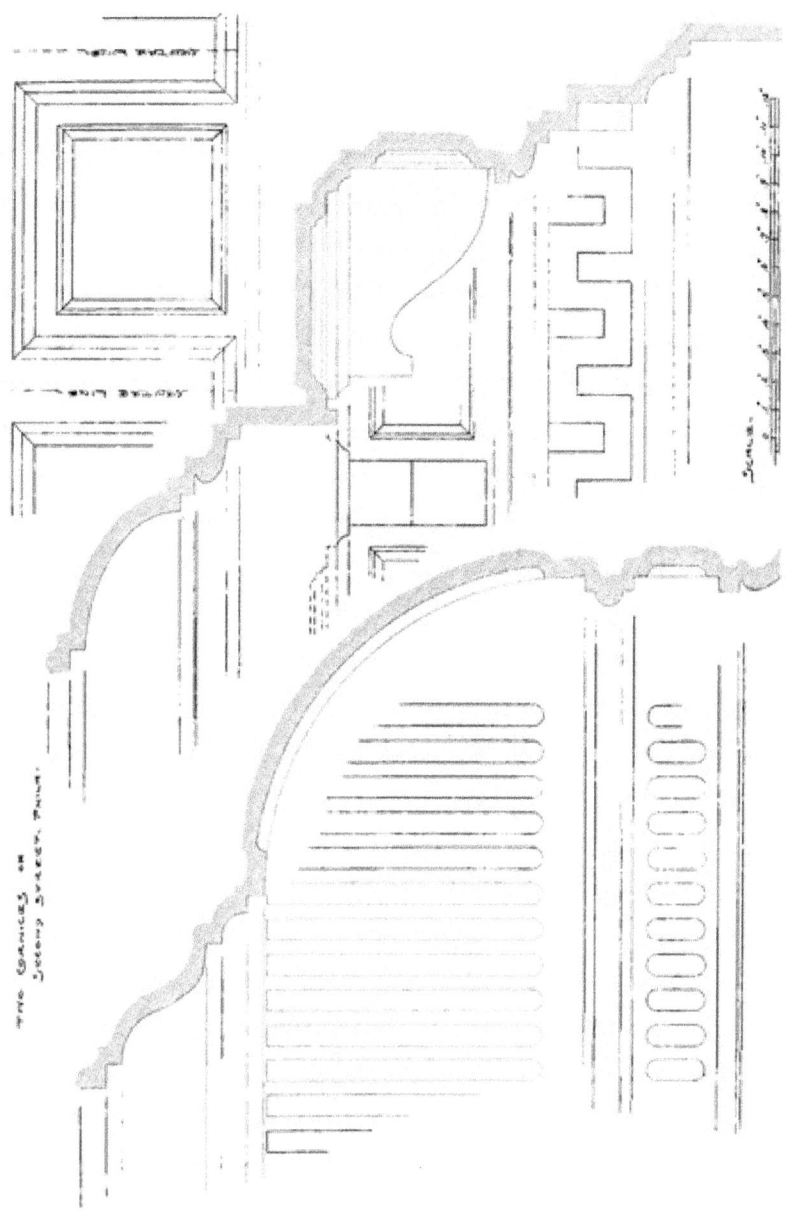

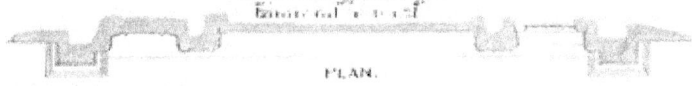

"OLD DOORWAY" 5TH AND POWEL STS. — PHILADA., PA.

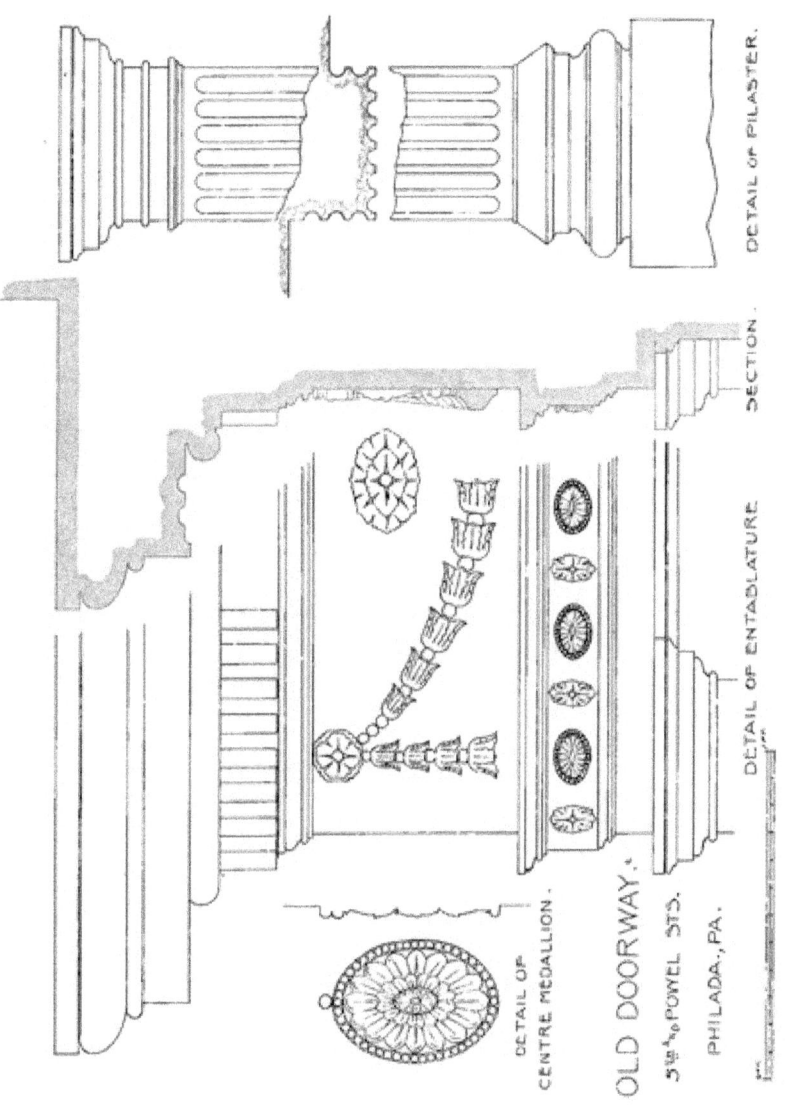

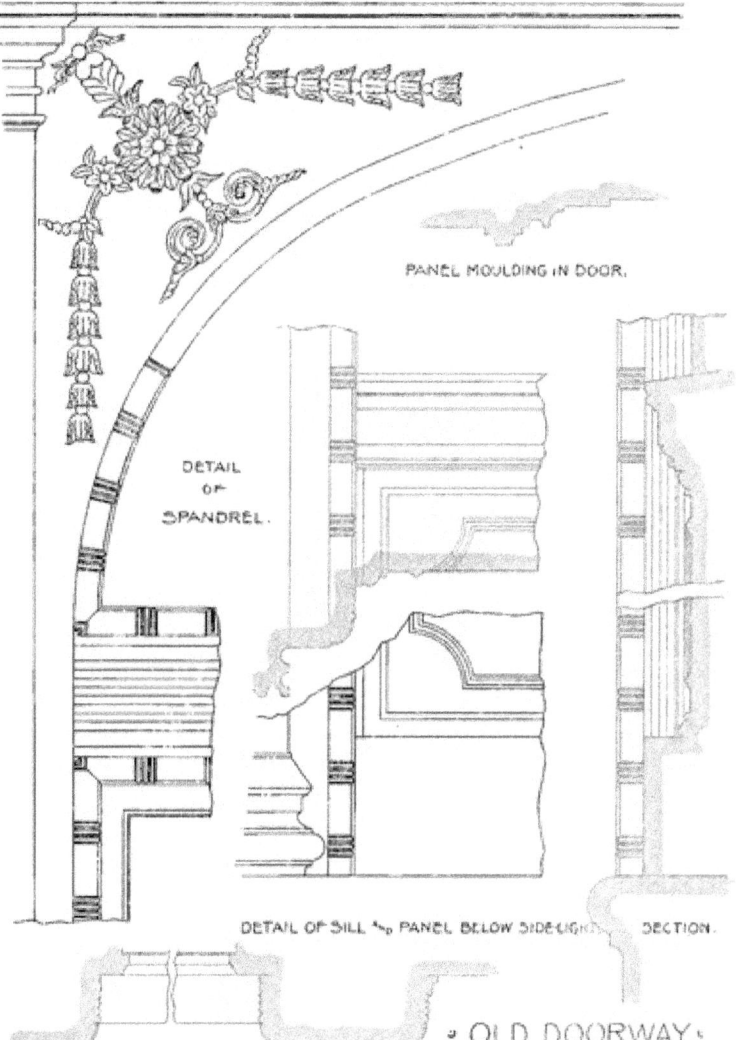

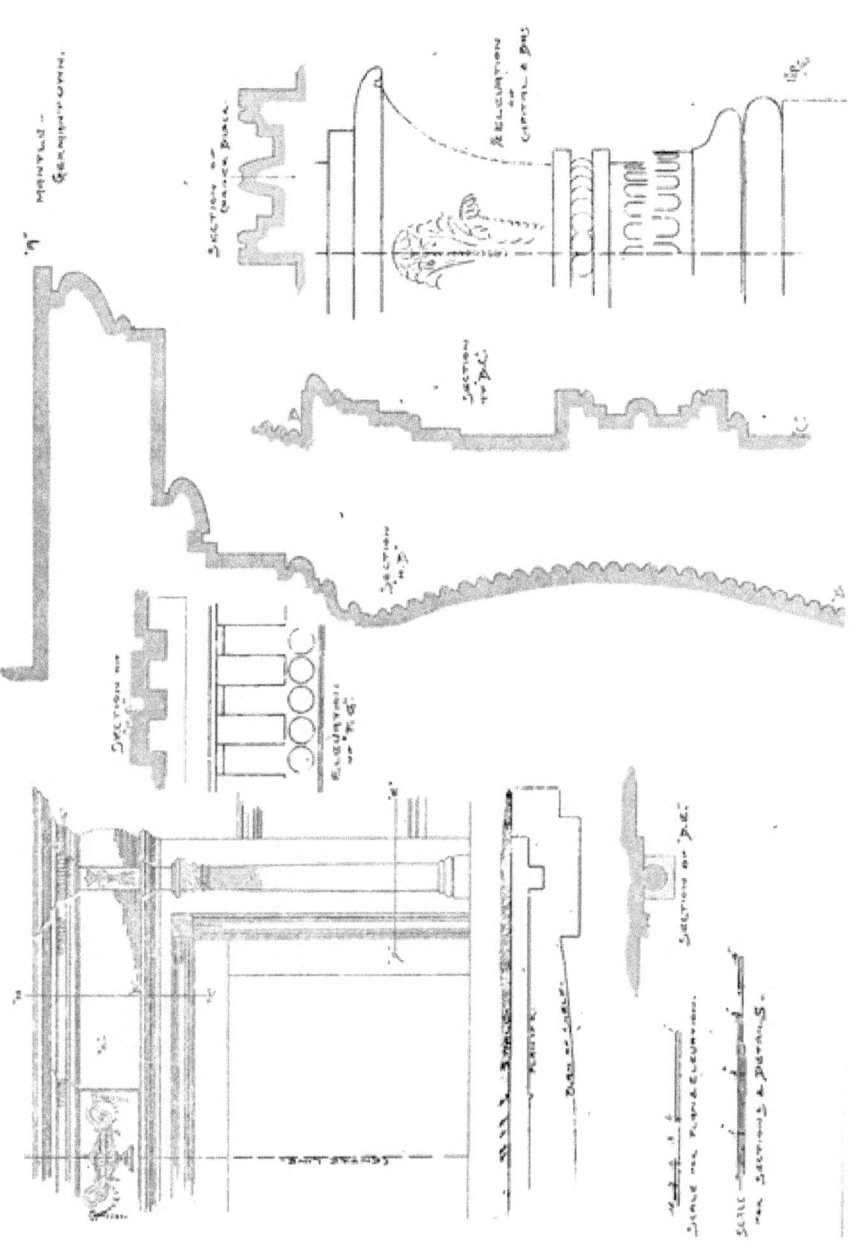

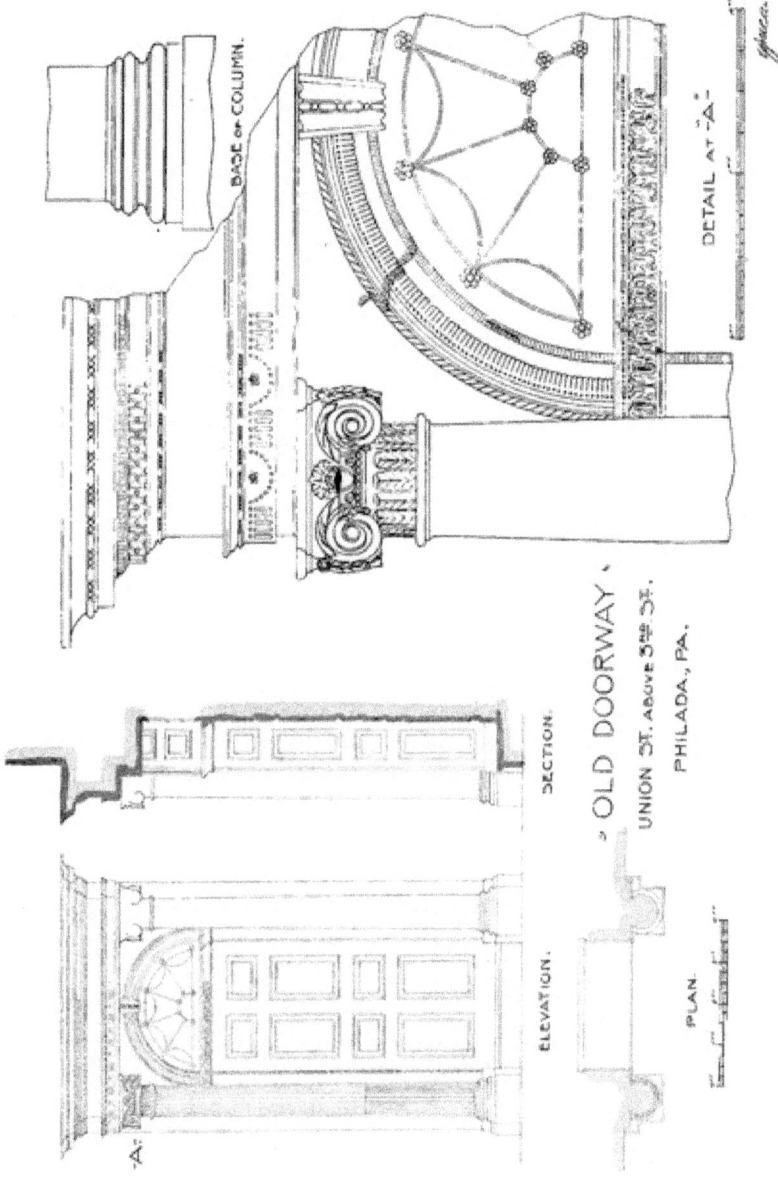

"OLD DOORWAY"
UNION ST. ABOVE 5TH ST.
PHILADA, PA.

"OLD DOORWAY" — LOCUST ST. BELOW 5TH ST., — PHILADA., PA. —

DETAIL OF PANEL IN DOOR.

BASE OF COLUMN.

DETAIL AT "C"

DETAIL OF MOULDING "D-D".

SECTION.

SECTION "A-A"

SECTION "D-D"

ELEVATION.

PLAN.

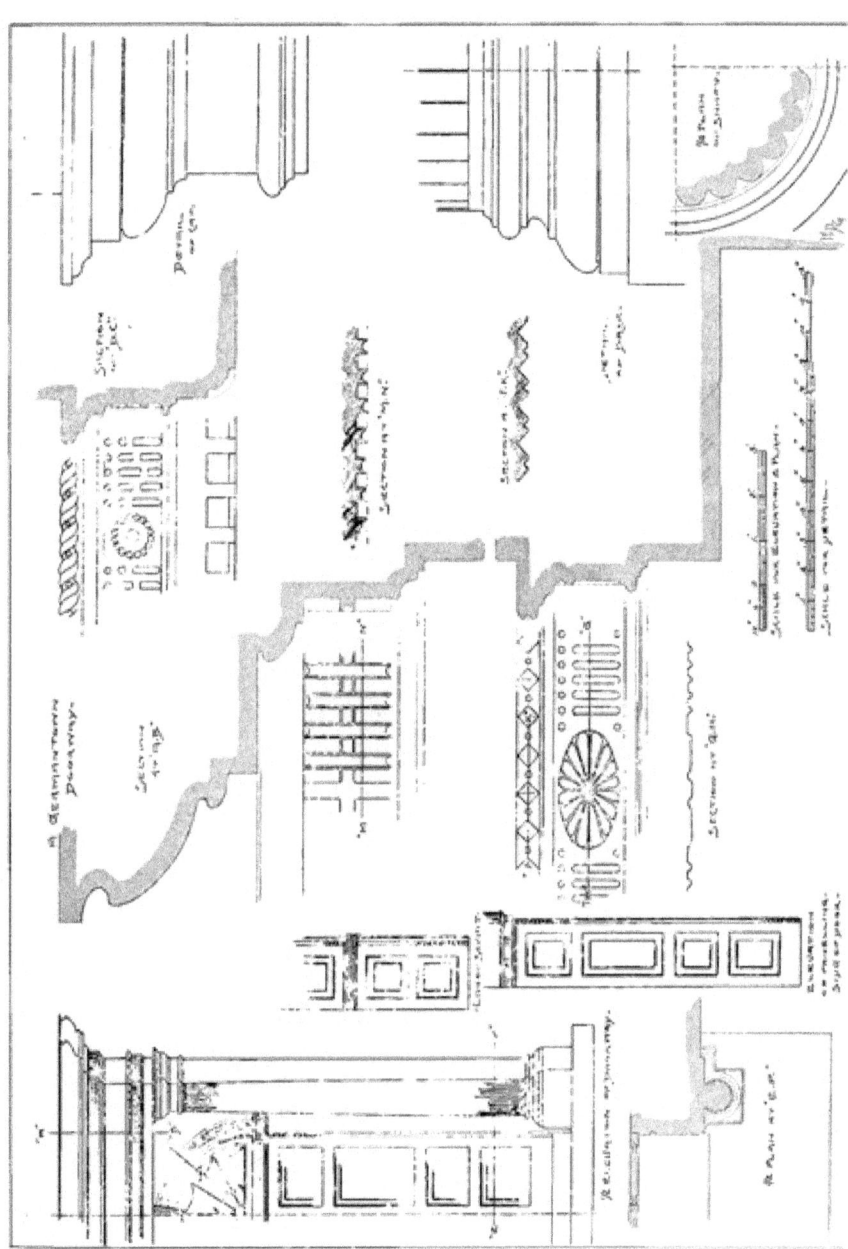

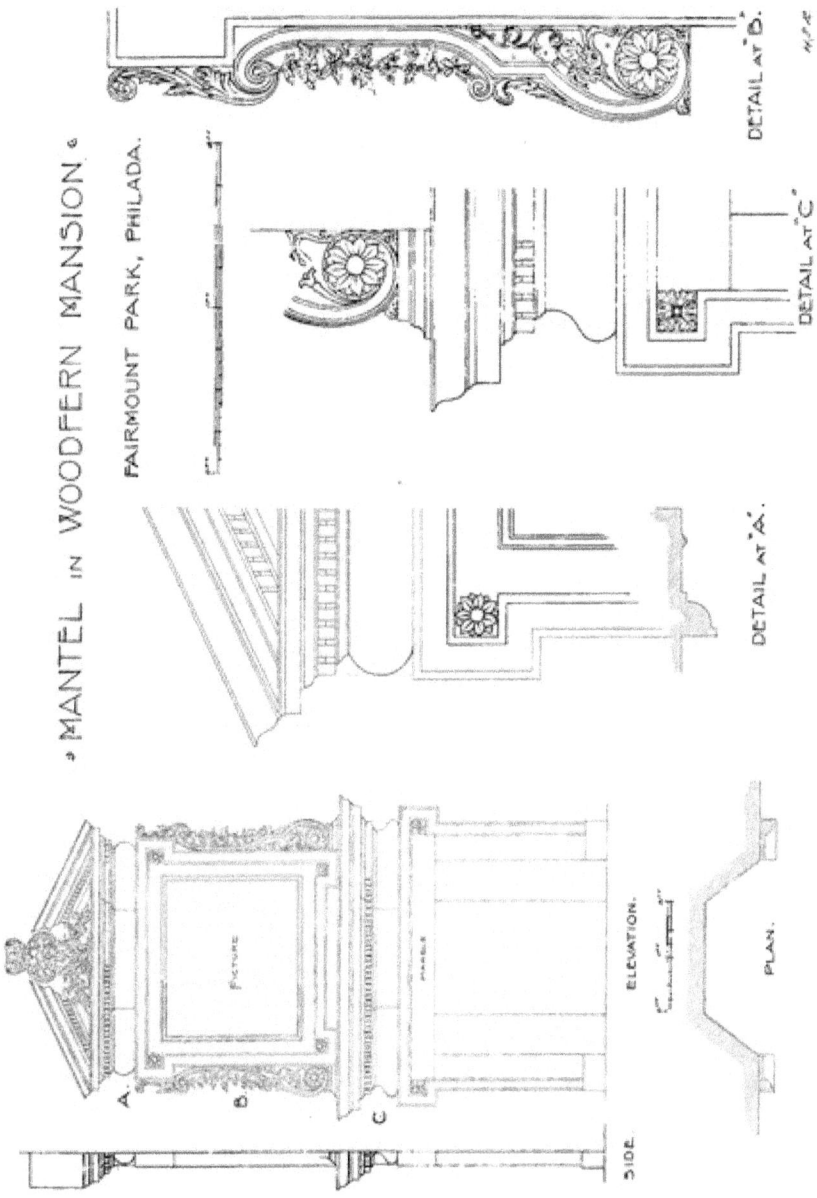

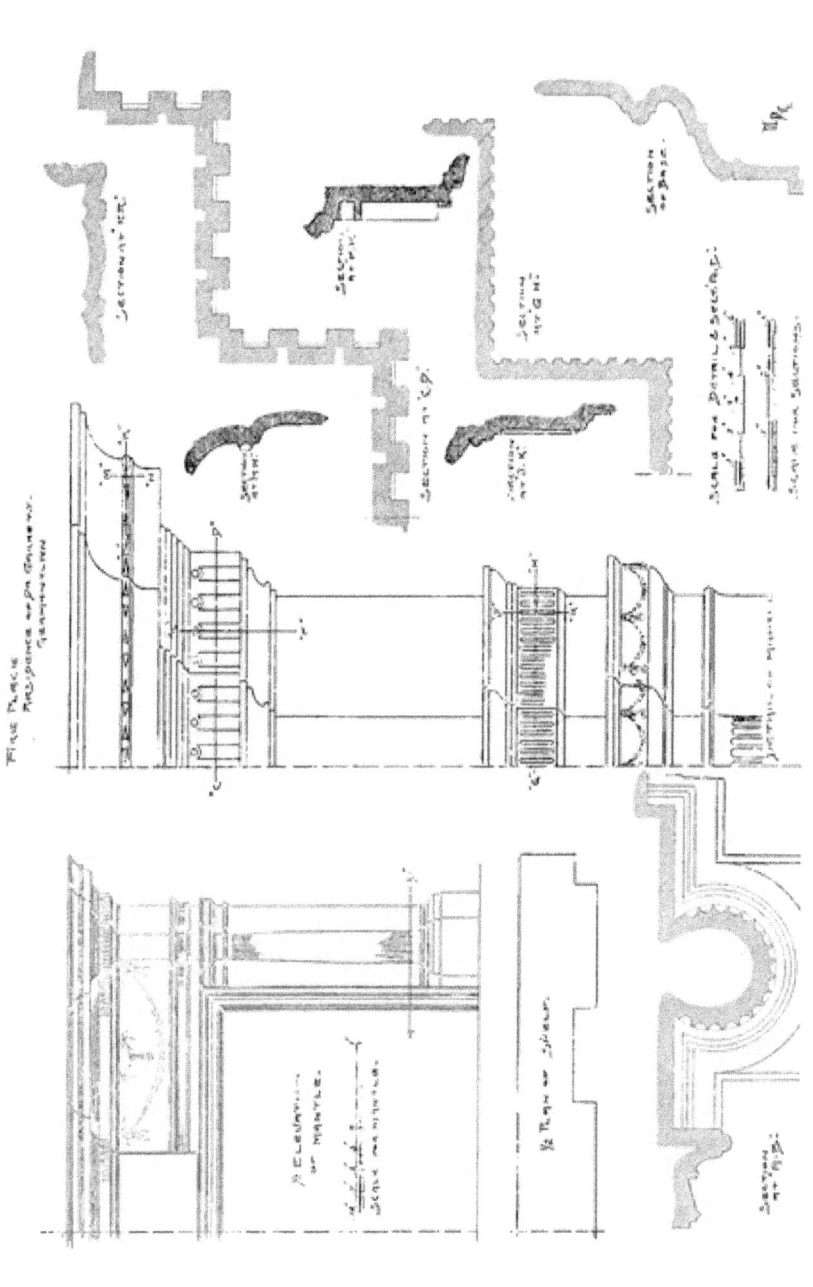

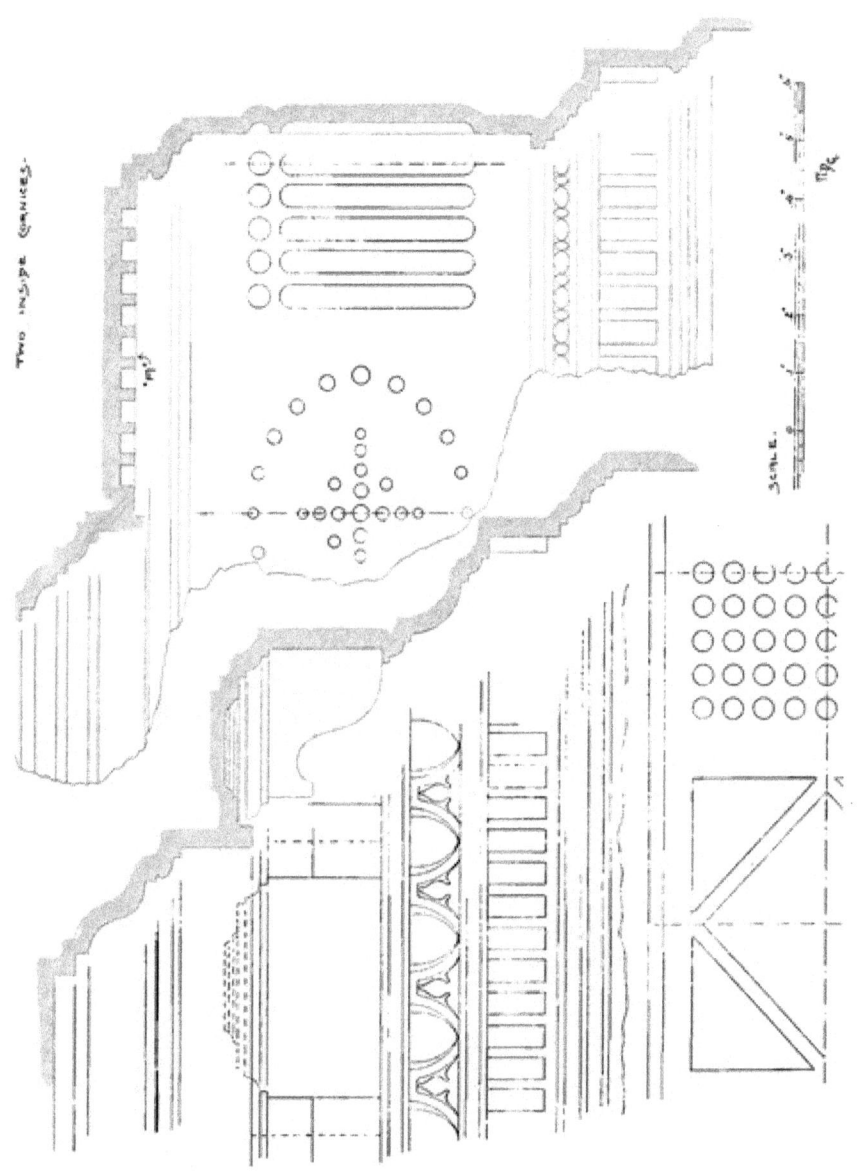

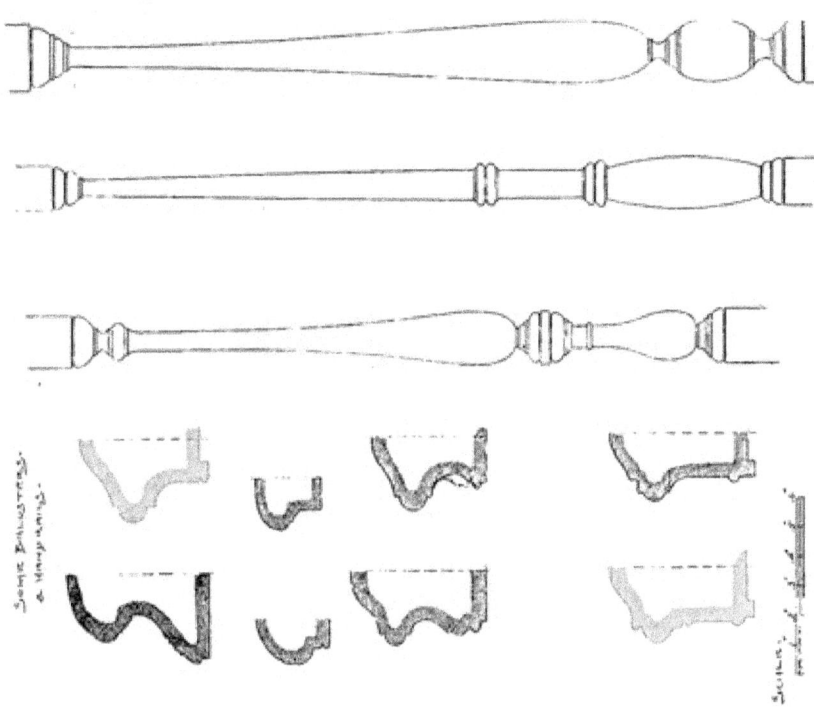

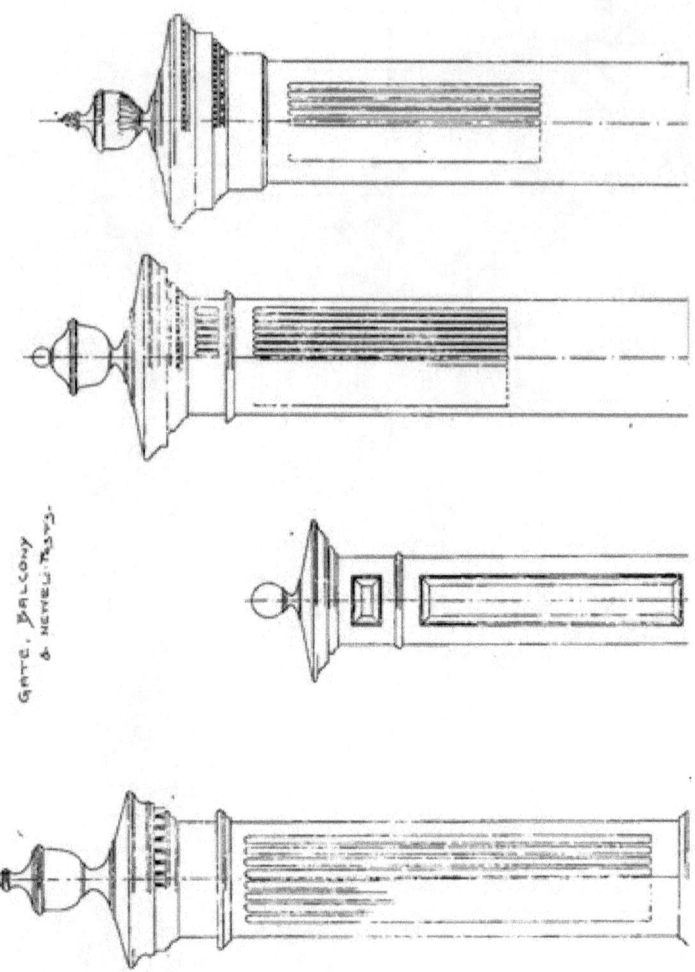

GATE, BALCONY & NEWEL POSTS.

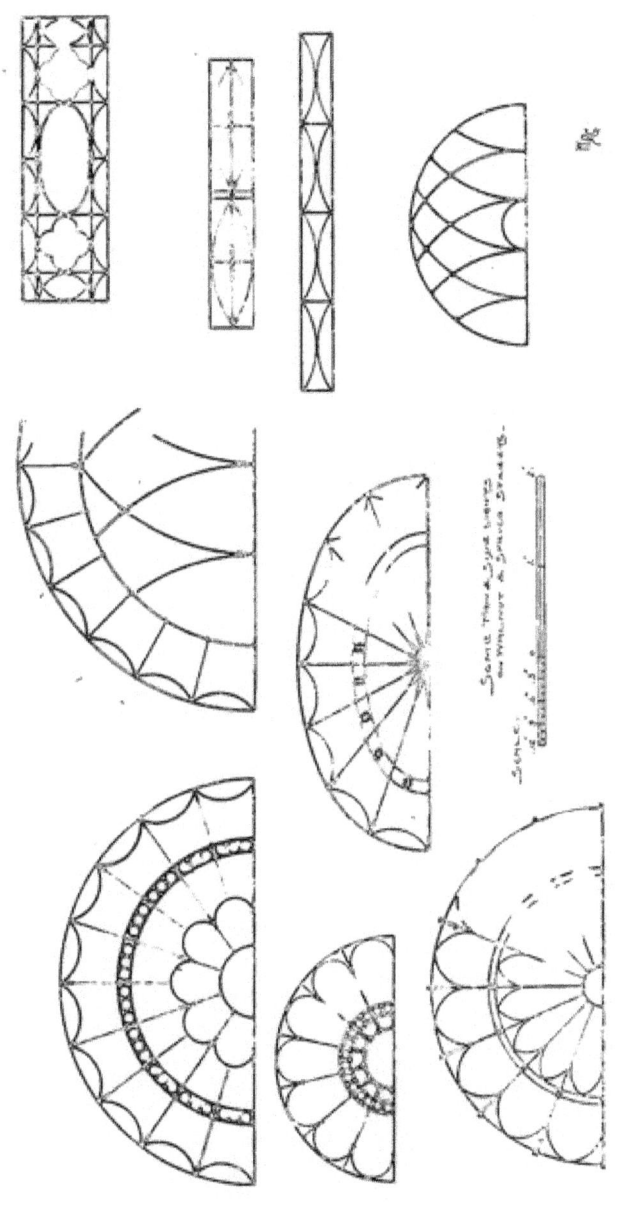

www.ingramcontent.com/pod-product-compliance
Lightning Source LLC
Chambersburg PA
CBHW031120160426
43192CB00008B/1052